His effigy was hung from the center light on Main Street. A cross was burned on the hill above his house. Hate-filled people whispered that he had been black all along.

This is a shocking book. It is the story of a man who underwent a series of medical treatments to change his skin color temporarily to black—a transformation that was complete when John Howard Griffin shaved off his hair, and looking in a mirror, saw a bald, middle-aged black man. From November 6th to December 14th, he hitchhiked, walked, and rode buses through Mississippi, Alabama, Louisiana, and Georgia. The experiences he encountered in the Deep South—the squalor, the violence, the antagonisms, the hopelessness—will burn deeply into the conscience of every American who believes in the justice of democracy.

"A stinging indictment of thoughtless, needless inhumanity. No one can read it without suffering."
—*Dallas News*

"*Black Like Me* is a moving and troubling book written by an accomplished novelist. It is a scathing indictment of our society."
—*Saturday Review*

BLACK LIKE ME

UPDATED WITH A NEW EPILOGUE BY THE AUTHOR

John Howard Griffin

A SIGNET BOOK

SIGNET
Published by the Penguin Group
Penguin Books USA Inc., 375 Hudson Street,
New York, New York 10014, U.S.A.
Penguin Books Ltd, 27 Wrights Lane,
London W8 5TZ, England
Penguin Books Australia Ltd, Ringwood,
Victoria, Australia
Penguin Books Canada Ltd, 10 Alcorn Avenue,
Toronto, Ontario, Canada M4V 3B2
Penguin Books (N.Z.) Ltd, 182–190 Wairau Road,
Auckland 10, New Zealand

Penguin Books Ltd, Registered Offices:
Harmondsworth, Middlesex, England

Published by Signet, an imprint of Dutton Signet,
a division of Penguin Books USA Inc.

Published by arrangement with Houghton Mifflin Company

Portions of this book first appeared in *Sepia* Magazine.
© Sepia Publishing Company, 1960

72 71 70 69 68 67

ⓓ REGISTERED TRADEMARK—MARCA REGISTRADA

Printed in the United States of America

BOOKS ARE AVAILABLE AT QUANTITY DISCOUNTS WHEN USED TO PROMOTE PROD-
UCTS OR SERVICES. FOR INFORMATION PLEASE WRITE TO PREMIUM MARKETING DIVI-
SION, PENGUIN BOOKS USA INC., 375 HUDSON STREET, NEW YORK, NEW YORK 10014.

PREFACE

This may not be all of it. It may not cover all the questions, but it is what it is like to be a Negro in a land where we keep the Negro down.

Some Whites will say this is not really it. They will say this is the white man's experience as a Negro in the South, not the Negro's.

But this is picayunish, and we no longer have time for that. We no longer have time to atomize principles and beg the question. We fill too many gutters while we argue unimportant points and confuse issues.

The Negro. The South. These are details. The real story is the universal one of men who destroy the souls and bodies of other men (and in the process destroy themselves) for reasons neither really understands. It is the story of the persecuted, the defrauded, the feared and detested. I could have been a Jew in Germany, a Mexican in a number of states, or a member of any "inferior" group. Only the details would have differed. The story would be the same.

This began as a scientific research study of the Negro in the South, with careful compilation of data for analysis. But I filed the data, and here publish the journal of my own experience living as a Negro. I offer it in all its crudity and rawness. It traces the changes that occur to heart and body and intelligence when a so-called first-class citizen is cast on the junkheap of second-class citizenship.

J. H. G.

Rest at pale evening . . .
A tall slim tree . . .
Night coming tenderly
        Black like me.

From "Dream Variation"
LANGSTON HUGHES

OCTOBER 28, 1959

For years the idea had haunted me, and that night it returned more insistently than ever.

If a white man became a Negro in the Deep South, what adjustments would he have to make? What is it like to experience discrimination based on skin color, something over which one has no control?

This speculation was sparked again by a report that lay on my desk in the old barn that served as my office. The report mentioned the rise in suicide tendency among Southern Negroes. This did not mean that they killed themselves, but rather that they had reached a stage where they simply no longer cared whether they lived or died.

It was that bad, then, despite the white Southern legislators who insisted that they had a "wonderfully harmonious relationship" with Negroes. I lingered on in my office at my parents' Mansfield, Texas, farm. My wife and children slept in our home five miles away. I sat there, surrounded by the smells of autumn coming through my open window, unable to leave, unable to sleep.

How else except by becoming a Negro could a white man hope to learn the truth? Though we lived side by side throughout the South, communication between the two races had simply ceased to exist. Neither really knew what went on with those of the other race. The Southern Negro will not tell the white man the truth. He long ago learned that if he speaks a truth unpleasing to the white, the white will make life miserable for him.

The only way I could see to bridge the gap between us was to become a Negro. I decided I would do this.

I prepared to walk into a life that appeared suddenly mysterious and frightening. With my decision to become a Negro I realized that I, a specialist in race issues, really knew nothing of the Negro's real problem.

▼ ▼ ▼

OCTOBER 29, 1959

I drove into Fort Worth in the afternoon to discuss the project with my old friend George Levitan. He is the owner of *Sepia,* an internationally distributed Negro magazine with a format similar to that of *Look.* A large, middle-aged man, he long ago won my admiration by offering equal job opportunities to members of any race, choosing according to their qualifications and future potentialities. With an on-the-job training program, he has made *Sepia* a model, edited, printed and distributed from the million-dollar Fort Worth plant.

It was a beautiful autumn day. I drove to his house, arriving there in midafternoon. His door was always open, so I walked in and called him.

An affectionate man, he embraced me, offered me coffee and had me take a seat. Through the glass doors of his den I looked out to see a few dead leaves floating on the water of his swimming pool.

He listened, his cheek buried in his fist as I explained the project.

"It's a crazy idea," he said. "You'll get yourself killed fooling around down there." But he could not hide his enthusiasm.

I told him the South's racial situation was a blot on the whole country, and especially reflected against us overseas;

and that the best way to find out if we had second-class citizens and what their plight was, would be to become one of them.

"But it'll be terrible," he said. "You'll be making yourself the target of the most ignorant rabble in the country. If they ever caught you, they'd be sure to make an example of you." He gazed out the window, his face puffed with concentration.

"But you know—it is a great idea. I can see right now you're going through with it, so what can I do to help?"

"Pay the tab and I'll give *Sepia* some articles—or let you use some chapters from the book I'll write."

He agreed, but suggested that before I made final plans I discuss it with Mrs. Adelle Jackson, *Sepia's* editorial director. Both of us have a high regard for this extraordinary woman's opinions. She rose from a secretarial position to become one of the country's distinguished editors.

After leaving Mr. Levitan, I called on her. At first she thought the idea was impossible. "You don't know what you'd be getting into, John," she said. She felt that when my book was published, I would be the butt of resentment from all the hate groups, that they would stop at nothing to discredit me, and that many decent whites would be afraid to show me courtesies when others might be watching. And, too, there are the deeper currents among even well-intentioned Southerners, currents that make the idea of a white man's assuming nonwhite identity a somewhat repulsive step down. And other currents that say, "Don't stir up anything. Let's try to keep things peaceful."

And then I went home and told my wife. After she recovered from her astonishment, she unhesitatingly agreed that if I felt I must do this thing, then I must. She offered, as her part of the project, her willingness to lead, with our three children, the unsatisfactory family life of a household deprived of husband and father.

I returned at night to my barn office. Outside my open window, frogs and crickets made the silence more profound. A chill breeze rustled dead leaves in the woods. It carried an odor of fresh-turned dirt, drawing my attention to the fields where the tractor had only a few hours ago stopped plowing the earth. I sensed the radiance of it in the stillness, sensed the earthworms that burrowed back into the depths of the furrows, sensed the animals that wandered in the woods in search of nocturnal rut or food. I felt the beginning loneliness, the terrible dread of what I had decided to do.

▼ ▼ ▼

OCTOBER 30, 1959

Lunched with Mrs. Jackson, Mr. Levitan, and three FBI men from the Dallas office. Though I knew my project was outside their jurisdiction and that they could not support it in any way, I wanted them to know about it in advance. We discussed it in considerable detail. I decided not to change my name or identity. I would merely change my pigmentation and allow people to draw their own conclusions. If asked who I was or what I was doing, I would answer truthfully.

"Do you suppose they'll treat me as John Howard Griffin, regardless of my color—or will they treat me as some nameless Negro, even though I am still the same man?" I asked.

"You're not serious," one of them said. "They're not going to ask you any questions. As soon as they see you, you'll be a Negro and that's all they'll ever want to know about you."

▼ ▼ ▼

NOVEMBER 1, 1959, NEW ORLEANS, LOUISIANA

Arrived by plane as night set in. I checked my bags at the Hotel Monteleone in the French Quarter and began walking.

Strange experience. When I was blind I came here and learned cane-walking in the French Quarter. Now, the most intense excitement filled me as I saw the places I visited while blind. I walked miles, trying to locate everything by sight that I once knew only by smell and sound. The streets were full of sightseers. I wandered among them, entranced by the narrow streets, the iron-grill balconies, the green plants and vines glimpsed in lighted flagstone courtyards. Every view was magical, whether it was a deserted, lamplit street corner or the neon hubbub of Royal Street.

I walked past garish bars where hawkers urged me in to see the "gorgeous girls" do their hip-shaking; and they left the doors open sufficiently to show dim, smoke-blue interiors crossed by long rays of pink spotlights that turned the seminude girls' flesh rose. I strolled on. Jazz blared from the bars. Odors of old stone and Creole cooking and coffee filled the streets.

At Broussard's, I had supper in a superb courtyard under the stars—*huîtres variées,* green salad, white wine and coffee; the same meal I had there in past years. I saw everything—the lanterns, the trees, the candlelit tables, the little fountain, as though I were looking through a fine camera lens. Surrounded by elegant waiters, elegant people and elegant food, I thought of the other parts of town where I would live in the days to come. Was there a place in New Orleans where a Negro could buy *huîtres variées?*

At ten I finished dinner and went to telephone an old friend who lives in New Orleans. He insisted I stay at his house, and I was relieved, for I foresaw all sorts of difficulties staying in a hotel while I turned into a Negro.

▼ ▼ ▼

NOVEMBER 2, 1959

In the morning I called the medical information service and asked for the names of some prominent dermatologists.

They gave me three names. The first one I called gave me an appointment immediately, so I took the streetcar to his office and explained my needs. He had had no experience with such a request, but was willing enough to aid me in my project. After taking my case history, he asked me to wait while he consulted with some of his colleagues by phone as to the best method of darkening my skin.

After some time he stepped back into the room and said they had all agreed we should attempt it with a medication taken orally, followed by exposure to ultraviolet rays. He explained they used it on victims of vitiligo, a disease that causes white spots to appear on the face and body. Until this medication was discovered, the victims of this disease had had to wear pancake make-up when they went out in public. It could be dangerous to use, however. It usually took from six weeks to three months to darken the skin pigmentation. I told him I could not spare that much time and we decided to try accelerated treatments, with constant blood tests to see how my system tolerated the medication.

I got the prescription filled, returned to the house and took the tablets. Two hours later I exposed my entire body to ultraviolet rays from a sun lamp.

My host remained away from the house most of the time. I told him I was on an assignment that I could not discuss and that he should not be surprised if I simply disappeared without saying good-by. I knew that he had no prejudices, but I nevertheless did not want to involve him in any way, since reprisals might be taken against him by bigots or by his associates, who might resent his role as my host once my story became known. He gave me a key to his house and we agreed to maintain our different schedules without worrying about the usual host-guest relationship.

After supper I took the trolley into town and walked through some of the Negro sections in the South Rampart-Dryades Street sections. They are mostly poor sections with cafés, bars and businesses of all sorts alongside cluttered residences. I searched for an opening, a way to enter the world of the Negro, some contact perhaps. As yet, it was a blank to me. My greatest preoccupation was that moment of transition when I would "pass over." Where and how would I do it? To get from the white world into the Negro world is a complex matter. I looked for the chink in the wall through which I might pass unobserved.

▼ ▼ ▼

NOVEMBER 6

For the past four days, I had spent my time at the doctor's or closed up in my room with cotton pads over my eyes and the sun lamp turned on me. They had made blood tests twice and found no indication of damage to the liver. But the medication produced lassitude and I felt constantly on the verge of nausea.

The doctor, well-disposed, gave me many warnings about the dangers of this project in so far as my contact with Negroes was concerned. Now that he had had time to think, he was beginning to doubt the wisdom of this course, or perhaps he felt strongly his responsibility. In any event, he warned me that I must have some contact in each major city so my family could check on my safety from time to time.

"I believe in the brotherhood of man," he said. "I respect the race. But I can never forget when I was an intern and had to go down on South Rampart Street to patch them up. Three or four would be sitting in a bar or at a friend's house. They were apparently friends one minute and then something would come up and one would get slashed up with a knife. We're willing enough to go all the way for them, but we've got this problem—how can you render the duties of justice to men when you're afraid they'll be so unaware of justice they may destroy you?—especially since their attitude toward their own race is a destructive one." He said this with real sadness. I told him my contacts indicated that Negroes themselves were aware of this dilemma and they were making strong efforts to unify the race, to condemn among themselves any tactic or any violence or injustice that would reflect against the race as a whole.

"I'm glad to hear that," he said, obviously unconvinced.

He also told me things that Negroes had told him—that the lighter the skin the more trustworthy the Negro. I was astonished to see an intelligent man fall for this cliché, and equally astonished that Negroes would advance it, for in effect it placed the dark Negro in an inferior position and fed the racist idea of judging a man by his color.

When not lying under the lamp, I walked the streets of New Orleans to orient myself. Each day I stopped at a sidewalk shoeshine stand near the French Market. The shine boy was an elderly man, large, keenly intelligent and a good talker. He had lost a leg during World War I. He showed none of the obsequiousness of the Southern Negro, but was polite and easy to know. (Not that I had any illusions that I knew him, for he was too astute to allow any white man that privilege.) I told him I was a writer, touring the Deep South to study living conditions, civil rights, etc., but I did not tell him I would do this as a Negro. Finally, we exchanged names. He was called Sterling Williams. I decided he might be the contact for my entry into the Negro community.

▼ ▼ ▼

NOVEMBER 7

I had my last visit with the doctor in the morning. The treatment had not worked as rapidly or completely as we had hoped, but I had a dark undercoating of pigment which I could touch up perfectly with stain. We decided I must shave my head, since I had no curl. The dosage was established and the darkness would increase as time passed. From there, I was on my own.

The doctor showed much doubt and perhaps regret that he had ever cooperated with me in this transformation. Again he gave me many firm warnings and told me to get in touch with him any time of the day or night if I got into trouble. As I left his office, he shook my hand and said gravely, "Now you go into oblivion."

A cold spell had hit New Orleans, so that lying under the lamp that day was a comfortable experience. I decided to shave my head that evening and begin my journey.

In the afternoon, my host looked at me with friendly alarm. "I don't know what you're up to," he said, "but I'm worried."

I told him not to be and suggested I would probably leave sometime that night. He said he had a meeting, but would cancel it. I asked him not to. "I don't want you here when I go," I said.

"What are you going to do—be a Puerto Rican or something?" he asked.

"Something like that," I said. "There may be ramifications. I'd rather you didn't know anything about it. I don't want you involved."

He left around five. I fixed myself a bite of supper and drank many cups of coffee, putting off the moment when I would shave my head, grind in the stain and walk out into the New Orleans night as a Negro.

I telephoned home, but no one answered. My nerves simmered with dread. Finally I began to cut my hair and shave my head. It took hours and many razor blades before my pate felt smooth to my hand. The house settled into silence around me. Occasionally, I heard the trolley car rattle past as the night grew late. I applied coat after coat of stain, wiping each coat off. Then I showered to wash off all the excess. I did not look into the mirror until I finished dressing and had packed my duffel bags.

Turning off all the lights, I went into the bathroom and closed the door. I stood in the darkness before the mirror, my hand on the light switch. I forced myself to flick it on.

In the flood of light against white tile, the face and shoulders of a stranger—a fierce, bald, very dark Negro—glared at me from the glass. He in no way resembled me.

The transformation was total and shocking. I had expected to see myself disguised, but this was something else. I was imprisoned in the flesh of an utter stranger, an unsympathetic one with whom I felt no kinship. All traces of the John Griffin I had been were wiped from existence.

Even the senses underwent a change so profound it filled me with distress. I looked into the mirror and saw reflected nothing of the white John Griffin's past. No, the reflections led back to Africa, back to the shanty and the ghetto, back to the fruitless struggles against the mark of blackness. Suddenly, almost with no mental preparation, no advance hint, it became clear and permeated my whole being. My inclination was to fight against it. I had gone too far. I knew now that there is no such thing as a disguised white man, when the black won't rub off. The black man is wholly a Negro, regardless of what he once may have been. I was a newly created Negro who must go out that door and live in a world unfamiliar to me.

The completeness of this transformation appalled me. It was unlike anything I had imagined. I became two men, the observing one and the one who panicked, who felt Negroid even into the depths of his entrails.

I felt the beginnings of great loneliness, not because I was a Negro but because the man I had been, the self I knew, was hidden in the flesh of another. If I returned home to my wife and children they would not know me. They would open the door and stare blankly at me. My children would want to know who is this large, bald Negro. If I walked up to friends, I knew I would see no flicker of recognition in their eyes.

I had tampered with the mystery of existence and I had lost the sense of my own being. This is what devastated me. The Griffin that was had become invisible.

The worst of it was that I could feel no companionship with this new person. I did not like the way he looked. Perhaps, I thought, this was only the shock of a first reaction. But the thing was done and there was no possibility of turning back. For a few weeks I must be this aging, bald Negro; I must walk through a land hostile to my color, hostile to my skin.

How did one start? The night lay out there waiting. A thousand questions presented themselves. The strangeness of my situation struck me anew——I was a man born old at midnight into a new life. How does such a man act? Where does he go to find food, water, a bed?

The phone rang and I felt my nerves convulse. I an-

swered and told the caller my host was out for the evening.
Again the strangeness, the secret awareness that the person
on the other end did not know he talked with a Negro.
Downstairs, I heard the soft chiming of the old clock. I
knew it was midnight though I did not count. It was time
to go.

With enormous self-consciousness I stepped from the
house into the darkness. No one was in sight. I walked to
the corner and stood under a street lamp, waiting for the
trolley.

I heard footsteps. From the shadows, the figure of a
white man emerged. He came and stood beside me. It was
all new. Should I nod and say "Good evening," or simply
ignore him? He stared intently at me. I stood like a statue,
wondering if he would speak, would question me.

Though the night was cold, sweat dampened my body.
This also was new. It was the first time this adult Negro had
ever perspired. I thought it vaguely illuminating that the
Negro Griffin's sweat felt exactly the same to his body as
the white Griffin's. As I had suspected they would be, my
discoveries were naïve ones, like those of a child.

The streetcar, with pale light pouring from its windows,
rumbled to a stop. I remembered to let the white man on
first. He paid his fare and walked to an empty seat, ignoring
me. I felt my first triumph. He had not questioned me. The
ticket-taker on the streetcar nodded affably when I paid my
fare. Though streetcars are not segregated in New Orleans,
I took a seat near the back. Negroes there glanced at me
without the slightest suspicion or interest. I began to feel
more confident. I asked one of them where I could find a
good hotel. He said the Butler on Rampart Street was as
good as any, and told me what bus to take from downtown.

I got off and began walking along Canal Street in the
heart of town, carrying one small duffel bag in each hand.
I passed the same taverns and amusement places where the
hawkers had solicited me on previous evenings. They were
busy, urging white men to come in and see the girls. The
same smells of smoke and liquor and dampness poured out
through half-open doors. Tonight they did not solicit me.
Tonight they looked at me but did not see me.

I went into a drugstore that I had patronized every day since my arrival. I walked to the cigarette counter where the same girl I had talked with every day waited on me.

"Package of Picayunes, please," I said in response to her blank look.

She handed them to me, took my bill and gave me change with no sign of recognition, none of the banter of previous days.

Again my reaction was that of a child. I was aware that the street smells, and the drugstore odors of perfume and arnica, were exactly the same to the Negro as they had been to the white. Only this time I could not go to the soda fountain and order a limeade or ask for a glass of water.

I caught the bus to South Rampart Street. Except for the taverns, the street was deserted when I arrived at the Butler Hotel. A man behind the counter was making a barbecue sandwich for a woman customer. He said he'd find me a room as soon as he finished. I took a seat at one of the tables and waited.

A large, pleasant-faced Negro walked in and sat at the counter. He grinned at me and said: "Man, you really got your top shaved, didn't you?"

"Yeah, doesn't it look all right?"

"Man, it's slick. Makes you look real good." He said he understood the gals were really going for bald-headed men. "They say that's a sure sign of being high-sexed." I let him think I'd shaved my head for that reason. We talked easily. I asked him if this were the best hotel in the area. He said the Sunset Hotel down the street might be a little better.

I picked up my bags and walked toward the door.

"See you around, Slick," he called after me.

An orange neon sign guided me to the Sunset Hotel, which is located next to a bar. The drab little lobby was empty. I waited a moment at the desk and then rang a call bell. A man, obviously awakened from sleep, came down the hall in his undershirt, buttoning on trousers. He said I would have to pay in advance and that he didn't allow men to take girls up to the rooms. I paid the $2.85 and he led me up narrow, creaking stairs to the second floor. I stood behind him as he opened the door to my room and saw over his shoulder the desolate, windowless cubicle. I almost backed out, but realized I could probably find nothing better.

We entered and I saw that the room was clean.

"The bathroom's down the hall," he said. I locked the door after him and sat down on the bed to the loud twang of springs. A deep gloom spread through me, heightened by noise of talk, laughter and juke-box jazz from the bar downstairs. My room was scarcely larger than the double bed. An open transom above the door into the hall provided the only ventilation. The air, mingled with that of other rooms, was not fresh. In addition to the bed, I had a tiny gas stove and a broken-down bed stand. On it were two thin hand towels, a half bar of Ivory soap.

It was past one now. The light was so feeble I could hardly see to write. With no windows I felt boxed in, suffocating.

I turned off my light and tried to sleep, but the noise was too much. Light through the open transom fell on the ceiling fan, casting distorted shadows of the four motionless blades against the opposite wall.

A dog barked nearby and his bark grew louder as another tune from the juke box blasted up through my linoleum floor. I could not shake the almost desperate sadness all this evoked, and I marveled that sounds could so degrade the spirit.

I slipped into my pants and walked barefoot down the narrow, dim-lit hall to the door with a crudely lettered sign reading MEN. When I stepped in, the hollow roar of water beating against the wall of a metal shower filled the room, along with an odor of cold sweat and soap. One man was in the shower. Another, a large, black-skinned man, sat naked on the floor awaiting his turn at the shower. He leaned back against the wall with his legs stretched out in front of him. Despite his state of undress, he had an air of dignity. Our eyes met and he nodded his polite greeting.

"It's getting cold, isn't it?" he said.

"It sure is."

"You talking to me?" the man in the shower called out above the thrumming.

"No—there's another gentleman here."

"I won't be much longer."

"Take your time—he don't want to shower."

I noted the bathroom was clean, though the fixtures were antique and rust-stained.

"Have you got a stove in your room?" the man on the floor asked. We looked at one another and there was kindness in his search for conversation.

"Yes, but I haven't turned it on."

"You *didn't* want to take a shower, did you?" he asked.

"No—it's too cold. You must be freezing on that bare floor, with no clothes on."

His brown eyes lost some of their gravity. "It's been so hot here recently. It feels kind of good to be cold."

I stepped over to the corner washbasin to rinse my hands.

"You can't use that," he said quickly. "That water'll run out on the floor." I looked beneath, as he indicated, and saw it had no drainpipe.

He reached beside him and flicked back the wet canvas shower curtain. "Hey, how about stepping back and letting this gentleman wash his hands?"

"That's all right, I can wait," I said.

"Go ahead," he nodded.

"Sure—come on," the man in the shower said. He turned the water down to a dribble. In the shower's obscurity, all I could see was a black shadow and gleaming white teeth. I stepped over the other's outstretched legs and washed quickly, using the soap the man in the shower thrust into my hands. When I had finished, I thanked him.

"That's all right. Glad to do it," he said, turning the water on full strength again.

The man on the floor handed up his towel for me to dry my hands. Under the dim light in the tiny room without windows, I realized I was having my first prolonged contact as a Negro with other Negroes. Its drama lay in its lack of drama, in its quietness, in the courtesies we felt impelled to extend to one another. I wondered if the world outside were so bad for us that we had to counter it among ourselves by salving one another with kindness.

"Do you want a cigarette?" I asked.

"Please sir—I believe I will." He leaned his heavy body

forward to accept one. His black flesh picked up dull high-
lights from the bare globe overhead. I fished in my pants
pocket for matches, and lighted our cigarettes. We talked
local politics. I told him I was new in town and knew nothing about them. He refrained from asking questions, but
explained that Mayor Morrison had a good reputation for
fairness and the Negroes were hoping he would get elected
governor. I sensed the conversation made little difference,
that for a few moments we were safe from the world and
we were loath to break the communication and go back to
our rooms. It gave us warmth and pleasure, though we
talked formally and showed one another great respect. Not
once did he ask my name or where I came from.

When the man in the shower finished and stepped out
dripping, the larger man hoisted himself up from the floor,
tossed his cigarette into the toilet bowl and got into the
shower. I told them good night and returned to my room,
less lonely, and warmed by the brief contact with others
like me who felt the need to be reassured that an eye could
show something besides suspicion or hate.

▼ ▼ ▼

NOVEMBER 8

The dark room. The streak of pale light through the
transom. I woke to it several times, thinking it a long night.
Then it occurred to me that there were no windows, that it
might well be day outside.

I dressed, took my bags and walked down the steps. The
sun glared brilliantly on Rampart Street. Traffic rushed past
the lobby window.

"You coming back tonight, Mr. Griffin?" the man at the
desk asked pleasantly.

"I'm not sure."

"You can leave your bags here if you wish."

"Thanks—I need what's in them," I said.

"Did you sleep all right?"

"Yes—fine. What time is it?"

"Little past eleven thiry."

"Damn. I think I did sleep."

The world looked blurred through the window and I waited for my eyes to accustom themselves to sunlight. I wondered what I should do, where I should go. I had a few changes of shirts, handkerchiefs and underwear in my duffel, about $200 in travelers checks and $20 in cash. In addition I had my medicines and a month's supply of the pigmentation capsules.

I stepped out into the street and began to walk in search of food.

No one noticed me. The street was full of Negroes. I ambled along, looking in store windows. White proprietors who cater exclusively to Negro trade stood in doorways and solicited us.

"Step right in—nice special in shoes today."

"Come in just a minute—no obligation—like to show you these new hats."

Their voices wheedled and they smiled in counterfeit.

It was the ghetto. I had seen them before from the high altitude of one who could look down and pity. Now I belonged here and the view was different. A first glance told it all. Here it was pennies and clutter and spittle on the curb. Here people walked fast to juggle the dimes, to make a deal, to find cheap liver or a tomato that was overripe. Here was the indefinable stink of despair. Here modesty was the luxury. People struggled for it. I saw it as I passed, looking for food. A young, slick-haired man screamed loud obscenities to an older woman on the sidewalk. She laughed and threw them back in his face. They raged. Others passed them, hearing, looking down, pursing lips, struggling not to notice.

Here sensuality was escape, proof of manhood for people who could prove it no other way. Here at noon, jazz blared from juke boxes and dark holes issued forth the cool odors of beer, wine and flesh into the sunlight. Here hips drew the eye and flirted with the eye and caused the eye to lust or laugh. It was better to look at hips than at the ghetto. Here I saw a young man, who carried in his body the substance of the saint, stagger, glass-eyed, unconscious from the dark hole, sit down on the curb and vomit between his feet.

"Man, he can't hold his a-tall," someone said.

I saw the sun caught in sweaty black wrinkles at the back of his neck as his head flopped forward.

"You okay?" I asked, bending over him.

He nodded listlessly.

"Yeah, shit, he's just gassed," someone said. "He's okay."

An odor of Creole cooking led me to a café at the corner. It was a small but cheerful room, painted baby blue. Tables were set with red-checked cloths. Except for a man at the counter, who nodded as I entered, I was the only customer. A pleasant young Negro woman took my order and fixed my breakfast: eggs, grits, bread and coffee—forty-nine cents—no butter and no napkin.

The man at the counter turned toward me and smiled, as though he wanted to talk. I had made it a rule to talk as little as possible at first. He noticed my bags and asked me if I were here looking for work. I told him I was and asked him if there were any better part of town where I could get a room.

"Ain't this awful?" He grimaced, coming over to my table.

"You live down here?"

"Yeah." He closed his eyes wearily. Light from the door struck gray in his temples.

"The Y over on Dryades is about the best place. It's clean and there's a nice bunch of fellows there," he said.

He asked me what kind of work I did and I told him I was a writer.

He told me that he often took the bus into the better parts of town where the whites lived, "just to get away from this place. I just walk in the streets and look at the houses . . . anything, just to get somewhere where it's decent . . . to get a smell of clean air."

"I know . . ." I sympathized.

I invited him to have a cup of coffee. He told me about the town, places where I might go to find jobs.

"Is there a Catholic church around here?" I asked after a while.

"Yeah—just a couple of blocks over on Dryades."

"Where's the nearest rest room?" I asked.

"Well, man, now just what do you want to do—piss or pray?" he chuckled. Though we talked quietly, the waitress heard, and her high chortle was quickly muffled in the kitchen.

"I guess it doesn't hurt for a man to do both once in a while," I said.

"You're so right," he laughed, shaking his head from side to side. "You're so right, sir. Lordy, Lordy . . . if you stick around this town, you'll find out you're going to end up doing most of your praying for a place to piss. It's not easy, I'm telling you. You can go in some of the stores around here, but you've almost got to buy something before you can ask them to let you use the toilet. Some of the taverns got places. You can go over to the train station or the bus station—places like that. You just have to locate them. And there's not many of them for us. Best thing's just to stick close to home. Otherwise sometimes you'll find you've got to walk halfway across town to find a place."

When I left him I caught the bus into town, choosing a seat halfway to the rear. As we neared Canal, the car began to fill with whites. Unless they could find a place to themselves or beside another white, they stood in the aisle.

A middle-aged woman with stringy gray hair stood near my seat. She wore a clean but faded print house dress that was hoisted to one side as she clung to an overhead pendant support. Her face looked tired and I felt uncomfortable. As she staggered with the bus's movement my lack of gallantry tormented me. I half rose from my seat to give it to her, but Negroes behind me frowned disapproval. I realized I was "going against the race" and the subtle tug-of-war became instantly clear. If the whites would not sit with us, let them stand. When they became tired enough or uncomfortable enough, they would eventually take seats beside us and soon see that it was not so poisonous after all. But to give them your seat was to let them win. I slumped back under the intensity of their stares.

But my movement had attracted the white woman's attention. For an instant our eyes met. I felt sympathy for her, and thought I detected sympathy in her glance. The exchange blurred the barriers of race (so new to me) long enough for me to smile and vaguely indicate the empty seat beside me, letting her know she was welcome to accept it.

Her blue eyes, so pale before, sharpened and she spat out, "What're you looking at me like *that* for?"

I felt myself flush. Other white passengers craned to look at me. The silent onrush of hostility frightened me.

"I'm sorry," I said, staring at my knees. "I'm not from here." The pattern of her skirt turned abruptly as she faced the front.

"They're getting sassier every day," she said loudly. Another woman agreed and the two fell into conversation.

My flesh prickled with shame, for I knew the Negroes rightly resented me for attracting such unfavorable attention. I sat the way I had seen them do, sphynxlike, pretending unawareness. Gradually people lost interest. Hostility drained to boredom. The poor woman chattered on, reluctant apparently to lose the spotlight.

I learned a strange thing—that in a jumble of unintelligible talk, the word "nigger" leaps out with electric clarity. You always hear it and always it stings. And always it casts the person using it into a category of brute ignorance. I thought with some amusement that if these two women only knew what they were revealing about themselves to every Negro on that bus, they would have been outraged.

I left the bus on Canal Street. Other Negroes aboard eyed me not with anger, as I had expected, but rather with astonishment that any black man could be so stupid.

For an hour, I roamed aimlessly through streets at the edge of the French Quarter. Always crowds and always the sun. On Derbigny Street I had coffee in a small Negro café called the Two Sisters Restaurant. A large poster on the wall caught my attention:

DESEGREGATE THE BUSES WITH THIS 7 POINT PROGRAM:
1. Pray for guidance.
2. Be courteous and friendly.
3. Be neat and clean.
4. Avoid loud talk.
5. Do not argue.

6. Report incidents immediately.
7. Overcome evil with good.
   Sponsored by Interdenominational
   Ministerial Alliance
   Rev. A. L. Davis, Pres.
   Rev. J. E. Poindexter, Secretary

I walked to the same shoeshine stand in the French Quarter that I had been visiting as a white man. My friend Sterling Williams sat on an empty box on the sidewalk. He looked up without a hint of recognition.

"Shine?"

"I believe so," I said and climbed up on the stand.

He hoisted his heavy body on his crutch and hobbled over to begin the work. I wore shoes of an unusual cut. He had shined them many times and I felt he should certainly recognize them.

"Well, it's another fine day," he said.

"Sure is."

I felt brisk strokes of his brush across the toe of my shoe.

"You're new in town, aren't you?"

I looked down on the back of his head. Gray hair kinked below the rim of a sea-captain cap of black canvas.

"Yeah—just been here a few days," I said.

"I thought I hadn't seen you around the quarter before," he said pleasantly. "You'll find New Orleans a nice place."

"Seems pretty nice. The people are polite."

"Oh . . . sure. If a man just goes on about his business and doesn't pay any attention to them, they won't bother you. I don't mean any bowing or scraping—just, you know, show you got some dignity." He raised his glance to my face and smiled wisely.

"I see what you mean," I said.

He had almost finished shining the shoes before I asked, "Is there something familiar about these shoes?"

"Yeah—I been shining some for a white man—"

"A fellow named Griffin?"

"Yeah." He straightened up. "Do you know him?"

"I am him."

He stared dumfounded. I reminded him of various subjects we had discussed on former visits. Finally convinced, he slapped my leg with glee and lowered his head. His shoulders shook with laughter.

"Well, I'm truly a son-of-a-bitch . . . how did you ever?"

I explained briefly. His heavy face shone with delight at what I had done and delight that I should confide it to him. He promised perfect discretion and enthusiastically began coaching me; but in a guarded voice, glancing always about to make sure no one could overhear.

I asked him if I could stay and help him shine shoes for a few days. He said the stand really belonged to his partner, who was out trying to locate some peanuts to sell to the winos of the quarter. We'd have to ask him, but he was sure it would be all right. "But you're way too well dressed for a shine boy."

We sat on boxes beside the stand. I asked him to check me carefully and tell me anything I did wrong.

"You just watch me and listen how I talk. You'll catch on. Say," he said excitedly, "you got to do something about those hands."

Sunlight fell on them, causing the hairs to glint against the black skin.

"Oh Lord," I groaned. "What'll I do?"

"You got to shave them," he said, holding up his large fist to show his own hand had no hairs. "You got a razor?"

"Yes."

"Hurry up, now, before somebody sees you." He became agitated and protective. "Down that alleyway there—clear to the end. You'll find a rest room. You can shave there right quick."

I grabbed my bag as he watched in agony to see that the way was clear. The shoe stand was in skid row—a street of ancient buildings with cheap rooming houses and bars.

I hurried to the alley and walked down it into the gloom of a cluttered courtyard. A few Negroes, who could not enter the white bar, were served from the back. They stood around or sat at wooden tables drinking. I saw a sign that read GENTLEMEN and was almost at the door when several voices shouted.

"Hey! You can't go in there. Hey!"

I turned back toward them, astonished that even among skid row derelict joints they had "separate facilities."

"Where do I go?" I asked.

"Clean on back there to the back," a large drunk Negro said, pointing with a wild swinging gesture that almost made him lose his balance.

I went another fifty feet down the alley and stepped into the wooden structure. It was oddly clean. I latched the door with a hook that scarcely held, smeared shaving cream on the backs of my hands and shaved without water.

Sterling nodded approval when I returned. He relaxed and smiled, the way one would after averting a terrible danger. His entire attitude of connivance was superbly exaggerated.

"Now there's not a hitch to you, my friend," he said. "Nobody'd ever guess."

An odd thing happened. Within a short time he lapsed into familiarity, forgetting I was once white. He began to use the "we" form and to discuss "our situation." The illusion of my "Negro-ness" took over so completely that I fell into the same pattern of talking and thinking. It was my first intimate glimpse. We were Negroes and our concern was the white man and how to get along with him; how to hold our own and raise ourselves in his esteem without for one moment letting him think he had any God-given rights that we did not also have.

A fine-looking middle-aged Negro woman, dressed in a white uniform, stepped out into the sidewalk a few doors away and stared at me.

Sterling nudged my ribs. "You got that widow woman interested," he laughed. "You just watch. She'll find some reason to come down here before long."

I asked him who she was.

"She works there in the bar—nice lady, too. She ain't going to rest till she finds out who you are."

I began to get thirsty and asked Sterling where I could find a drink.

"You've got to plan ahead now," he said. "You can't do like you used to when you were a white man. You can't just walk in anyplace and ask for a drink or use the rest room. There's a Negro café over in the French Market about two blocks up. They got a fountain in there where you can drink. The nearest toilet's the one you just came from. But here—I got water."

He reached behind the shine stand and brought out a gallon lard can with wires looped through holes in each side to make a handle. A flake of ash floated on the water's surface. I up-ended the bucket and drank.

"Well, well, we're going to have company," Sterling said. "That nice widow woman's coming this way."

I glanced down the street. Past the metal upright shoe racks I saw her walk gracefully toward us. She was carefully looking across the street.

She ignored me and asked Sterling if he had any peanuts to sell.

"No, dear heart. Joe's out looking for some now. They're hard to find this time of year." He spoke unctuously, as though he had no idea why she really came down; but all three of us knew he knew and that we knew he knew. But the game had to be played.

Then she turned and saw me, apparently for the first time. She looked startled, then delighted. "Why how do you do?" she said with a magnificent smile that illuminated not only her face but the entire quarter.

I bowed and returned the smile, spontaneously, because the radiance of her expression took me by surprise. "Why, just fine. How do you do?"

"Fine," she bowed. "Nice to see you around."

I bowed again, confused. "I thank you, daughter."

After an awkward, grin-filled pause, she turned to walk away. "Well, I'll be seeing you," she sang out over her shoulder.

I looked dumbly at Sterling. He lifted his cap and scratched into the gray hairs of his head, his eyes wise and wide with amusement.

"Did you get that, eh?" he asked. "She liked you. You're in a fix now." He burst out laughing. "You hadn't counted on something like *that*, eh?"

"I sure hadn't," I said.

"She ain't no slut," he said. "She's a widow looking for a mate, and you're well dressed. She ain't going to pass up a chance like that."

"Oh Lord—this complicates things," I groaned. "Tell her I'm already married, will you?"

"Well, now, I don't know," he smiled. "That might just spoil the fun. I think I'll just tell her you're a widow man, a preacher visiting here in New Orleans. I feel like she's the kind that would love to be a preacher's wife."

"Look—you know I can't fiddle around with things like that. It'll be no fun for her when this project gets known and she finds out I'm a white man."

Customers came—whites, Negroes and Latin Americans. Well-dressed tourists mingled with the derelicts of the quarter. When we shined their shoes we talked. The whites, especially the tourists, had no reticence before us, and no shame since we were Negroes. Some wanted to know where they could find girls, wanted us to get Negro girls for them. We learned to spot these from the moment they sat down, for they were immediately friendly and treated us with the warmth and courtesy of equals. I mentioned this to Sterling.

"Yeah, when they want to sin, they're very democratic," he said.

Though not all, by any means, were so open about their purposes, all of them showed us how they felt about the Negro, the idea that we were people of such low morality that nothing could offend us. These men, young and old, however, were less offensive than the ones who treated us like machines, as though we had no human existence whatsoever. When they paid me, they looked as though I were a stone or a post. They looked and saw nothing.

Sterling's partner, Joe, returned from his peanut hunt around two. We explained my presence and he welcomed me. Slender, middle-aged, though he looked young, Joe impressed me as a sharp but easygoing man. He lamented the lack of peanuts. Sterling told him many drunks had stopped by wanting to buy some and that they could have made a pocketful of change had they been able to supply them.

Joe began to cook our lunch on the sidewalk. He put paper and kindling from an orange crate into a gallon can and set it afire. When the flames had reduced to coals, he placed a bent coat hanger over the top as a grill and set a pan on it to heat. He squatted and stirred with a spoon. I learned it was a mixture of coon, turnips and rice, seasoned with thyme, bay leaf and green peppers. Joe had cooked it at home the night before and brought it in a milk carton. When it was heated through, Joe served Sterling and me portions in cut-down milk cartons. He ate directly from the pan. It was good, despite the odor of rot that smoked up from it.

Joe leaned over to me and pointed with his spoon to a man across the street. "Watch that wino," he said. "He'll sit right there—he wants some of this food, but he won't come over till I tell him to."

Sitting on the curb across the street, the man stared feverishly at us, tensed, ready to come for the food when called. His eyes burned in his black face and his fists were doubled hard, as though he had to control himself from rushing over and grabbing the food.

We ate slowly while the man stared. It was a strange game. We, who were reduced to eating on the sidewalk, were suddenly elevated in status by this man's misery. We were the aristocrats and he the beggar. It flattered us. We were superbly above him and the comedy gave us a delusion of high self-respect. In a while, the magnanimity of the rich would complete the picture. We would feed our scraps to the poor.

Our servings were ample. When we had eaten our fill, we scraped the remains from our cartons into Joe's plate.

The man trembled with expectation as Joe leisurely smoothed the food with the back of his spoon. Then, without looking at the wretch, Joe held out the pan. In a strangely kind tone of voice he said: "Okay, dog ass, come get some food."

The man bolted across the street and grabbed the pan.

"If there'd been a car coming, he'd have been killed," Sterling remarked.

"Now, listen, winehead—I want that pan back *clean*, you hear?" Joe said.

The beggar's gaze riveted to the food, his face crumpled as though he were about to weep and he hurried into the alley without answering.

"He comes here every day . . . it's the same thing," Sterling said. "I guess he'd starve if it weren't for Joe."

Business died. We sat on boxes in the sunlight with our backs against the wall and watched traffic come and go in the French Market. I stared into the broken windows of a deserted stone building across the street. Sterling snored loudly and then awoke with a strangled snort.

The beggar returned the pan, still wet from being washed. He handed it to Joe.

"Okay, winehead," Joe said.

Without speaking, the man drifted away.

I listened to the easy and usually obscene give-and-take between Joe and men of the quarter who passed the sidewalk.

"Hey, dog nuts, what's your hurry?"

"I got business, man."

"What business you got? Hey—where can I get some peanuts?"

"They ain't a peanut in this whole town. I been all over."

"Me, too," Joe said.

Odors of sweat, tobacco, coffee and damp stone surrounded us, overladen always by the smell of fish and nearby salt water.

I felt the wall warm against my back, making me drowsy. My first afternoon as a Negro was one of dragging hours and a certain contentment.

After a while Joe took a pocket Bible from the green serge army shirt he wore and began reading the Psalms to himself. His eyes drooped but he formed the words silently with his lips. From force of long habit, whenever anyone walked by, he said "Shine?" without raising his head from the page.

Two pigeons flew down to the sidewalk at our feet. Joe tossed them some bread scraps. The sun sparked iridescence from their purple necks as they pecked. They provided us deep pleasure, an anodyne to the squalor and clutter of the street.

Joe got stiffly up, dusted his seat and ambled across to the fish market. When he returned, he had a sack of catfish heads and some green bananas. He told me the catfish heads were free and that tomorrow we would have them for lunch—catfish-head stew over spaghetti.

"It sounds good," I said, looking into the sack at dozens of glittering eyes.

We wrapped the green bananas he had retrieved from the market waste-bins in newspapers. "They'll be ripe enough to eat in about two or three days," he said.

By four o'clock the street was in shadow. Sunlight rimmed the buildings above us and the air chilled rapidly. I decided to go find a room for the night. Sterling suggested I go to the Negro YMCA on Dryades, some distance across town.

"You better drink some water before you go," he said. "You might not find any before you get to Dryades." I upended the bucket and saw the brass-colored circles at the bottom through the clear water.

A bluish haze hung over the narrow streets of the French Quarter. The strong odor of roasting coffee overwhelmed all others. The aroma and the scene reminded me of my school days in France. This was like the old quarter of Tours where they roasted coffee at the spice shops each afternoon.

I emerged on Canal Street to a more modern scene, a crowded scene. I deliberately stopped many white men to ask the direction to Dryades in order to get their reaction. Invariably they were courteous and helpful.

On Dryades, the whites thinned and I saw more and more Negroes in the street. A church came into view on my right, its tower rising up past a bridge heavy with traffic. A sign told me it was St. John the Baptist Catholic Church, one of the oldest in New Orleans. I mounted the steps and pulled open one of the heavy doors. Street noises were muffled with its closing. A faint fragrance of incense drifted to me in the deep silence. Soft, warm light filtered through magnificent stained-glass windows in the church proper. Far to the front I saw the dim figure of a Negro woman making the Stations of the Cross. A few men knelt here and there in the vast structure. Votive candles burned feebly in blue and red clusters before statues of St. Joseph and the Virgin Mary. I rested in a pew, leaning forward, my forehead against the bench in front, my hands in my lap. At home my wife and children were probably having their evening baths, safe against the dusk and the cold. I thought of the house, so full of light and talk, and wondered what they would have for supper. Perhaps even now soup simmered on the kitchen stove. Opening my eyes, I looked down at my hands and saw each dark pore, each black wrinkle in the hairless flesh. How white by contrast the image came to me of my wife and children. Their faces, their flesh simmered with whiteness and they seemed so much a part of another life, so separated from me now that I felt consumed with loneliness. Rosary beads rattled against one of the pews, loud in the stillness. Perceptibly the light dimmed through the windows and the candles grew brighter.

Dreading the thought of spending another night in some cheap hotel if I could not get a room at the Y, I considered hiding in the church and sleeping there in one of the pews. The idea appealed to me so strongly I had to cast it off by force. I got to my feet and walked out into a dusk shot with car lights rushing in each direction.

The YMCA was filled to capacity, but the young man behind the desk suggested they had a list of nice homes where a man could rent a room. He kindly offered to telephone some of these. While waiting, I had a cup of coffee in the YMCA Coffee Shop, an attractive, modern place run by an elderly man who spoke with great elegance and courtesy. The young man at the desk came and told me he had arranged for a room in a private home next door to the Y. He assured me it was nice there, and that the widow who owned it was trustworthy in every way.

I carried my bags next door and met Mrs. Davis, a middle-aged woman of great kindness. She led me upstairs to a back room that was spotlessly clean and comfortably furnished. We arranged for a brighter lamp so I could work. She told me she had only one other roomer, a quiet gentleman who worked nights and whom I should probably never see. The kitchen was next to my room, and beyond that the bathroom. I paid the three-dollar charge in advance, unpacked and returned to the YMCA Coffee Shop, which turned out to be the meeting place of the city's important men. There I met a much more educated and affluent class, older men who brought me into the conversation. We sat around a U-shaped counter drinking coffee. The talk was focused exclusively on "the problem" and the forthcoming elections. The café proprietor introduced me to the Reverend A. L. Davis and one of his colleagues, Mr. Gayle, a civic leader and bookstore-owner, and a number of others.

My feeling of disorientation diminished for a time.

When asked what I did, I told them I was a writer, touring the South to make a study of conditions.

"Well, what do you think?" the Reverend Mr. Davis asked.

"I've only begun," I said. "But so far it's much better than I expected to find. I've been shown many courtesies by the whites."

"Oh, we've made strides," he said. "But we've got to do a lot better. Then, too, New Orleans is more enlightened than anyplace else in the state—or in the South."

"Why is that, I wonder?" I asked.

"Well, it's far more cosmopolitan, for one thing. And it's got a strong Catholic population," he said. "A white man can show you courtesies without fearing some neighbor will call him a 'nigger-lover' like they do in other places."

"What do you see as our biggest problem, Mr. Griffin?" Mr. Gayle asked.

"Lack of unity."

"That's it," said the elderly man who ran the café. "Until we as a race can learn to rise together, we'll never get anywhere. That's our trouble. We work against one another instead of together. Now you take dark Negroes like you, Mr. Griffin, and me," he went on. "We're old Uncle Toms to our people, no matter how much education and morals we've got. No, you have to be almost a mulatto, have your hair conked and all slicked out and look like a Valentino. Then the Negro will look up to you. You've got *class.* Isn't that a pitiful hero-type?"

"And the white man knows that," Mr. Davis said.

"Yes," the café-owner continued. "He *utilizes* this knowledge to flatter some of us, tell us we're above our people, not like most Negroes. We're so stupid we fall for it and work against our own. Why, if we'd work just half as hard to boost our race as we do to please whites whose attentions flatter us, we'd really get somewhere."

A handsome, mature man entered and was introduced as J. P. Guillory, an insurance agent. When the others had gone and the café was closing, Mr. Guillory told me he came often to the Y to play chess. He asked if I would join him in a game, but I had work to do.

"Your name is somehow familiar, Mr. Griffin," he said. "I'm an avid reader. I must have read something by you. What are the names of some of your books?"

I named them. His face blanked with astonishment.

"Why, I just started reading that. My lawyer friend lent it to me," he said. He gazed at me and I had no doubt he thought I was either a tremendous liar for claiming authorship of a white man's book or that I was confessing something to him.

"I promise you I wrote it," I said. "I can't tell you more, but read the book, and the piece in last September *Reader's Digest* and you'll know who I really am."

I returned to my room and wrote in my journal. My landlady lit the fire and brought a pitcher of drinking water for my night stand. As I looked up to thank her, I saw the image in the large mirror of the wardrobe. Light gleamed from the elderly Negro's head as he looked up to talk to the Negro woman. The sense of shock returned; it was as though I were invisible in the room, observing a scene in which I had no part.

I dozed and the phone awakened me. I listened to it ring again and again but then realized that it could not be for me. No one in the world knew where I was. Finally someone answered it.

I heard noise and laughter. I got up in the darkness and walked to the window that looked down into the windows of the Y gym. Two Negro teams were playing baseball and a crowd of spectators alternately booed and cheered their favorites. I sat at the window and watched them until hunger began to pester me.

The kitchen clock read 7:30 when I passed through to go out to eat. I walked over to South Rampart in search of a café. As I turned the corner, I noticed two large white boys sprawled on the front steps of a house across the wide boulevard. One of them, a heavy-set, muscular fellow in khaki pants and a white sweat shirt, whistled at me. I ignored him and continued walking. From the corner of my eye, I saw him get slowly to his feet and angle across under the street light to my side of the street.

"Hey, Baldy," he called softly.

I walked faster and looked straight ahead.

"Hey, Mr. No-Hair," he called. I realized he was following about seventy-five feet behind me. He spoke casually, almost pleasantly, his voice clear in the deserted street.

"I'm going to get you, Mr. No-Hair. I'm after you. There ain't no place you go I won't get you. If it takes all night, I'll get you—so count on it."

A deep terror took me. I walked faster, controlling my desire to break into a run. He was young, strong. If I made it a chase, he would easily overtake me.

His voice drifted to me again, from about the same distance, soft and merciless. "Ain't no way you can get away from me, Mr. Shithead. You might as well stop right there."

I did not answer, did not turn. He stalked me like a cat.

Cars passed occasionally. I prayed that a police car might choose this street. I noted that when my footsteps slowed, his slowed; when mine accelerated, his matched them. I looked for an open door, a light. The stores were closed. The sidewalk, with grass at each seam, stretched ahead from street lamp to street lamp.

Then, to my immense relief, I saw an elderly couple waiting on the corner for a bus. I approached and they stiffened with caution. The quarter was not safe at night.

I glanced back to see the boy halted at mid-block, leaning against the wall.

"I'm in trouble," I said to the couple.

They ignored me.

"Please," I said. "Someone's chasing me. I don't know

what he wants, but he says he'll get me. Is there anyplace around here where I can call the police?"

The man looked around. "Who's chasing you, mister?" he asked irritably.

"That boy back there . . ." I turned and pointed to the empty street. The boy had disappeared.

The man grunted disapprovingly, as though he thought I were drunk.

I waited for a moment, thinking I would catch the bus. Then, certain it had been only a prank, I started down the side street toward well-lighted Dryades, where I knew I would be safe.

I had gone only half a block when I heard the voice again.

"Hey, Shithead," he said quietly.

I tasted fear and despair like salt in my mouth.

"You can stop right along about there anyplace, dad."

We walked on in silence, his footsteps again matching mine.

"Stop right along there. Ain't no nice people on this street for you to hide behind, Baldy."

I searched for some solution and could find none. Something deadly, nightmarish about the pursuit terrified me more than the pursuit itself. I wondered about my family. What if he should knock me in the head—or worse; he sounded diabolic. For an instant I imagined the expression on some police officer's face as he looked at my black body and read my identification papers:

> JOHN HOWARD GRIFFIN
> MANSFIELD, TEXAS
> Weight: 196
> Hair: Brown
> Race: *White*
> Sex: Male
> Height: 6'1½"

Would he think I had merely stolen the papers from some white man?

"What do you keep walking for when I told you to stop, dad?"

I knew I should never get away from the bully unless I bluffed. I had long ago been trained in judo. Perhaps if I were lucky enough to get in the first blow, I might have a chance. I saw an alleyway in the dim light and summoned a deep growl.

"You come on, boy," I said without looking back. "You follow me, boy. I'm heading into that alley down there."

We walked on.

"That's right, boy," I said. "Now you're doing just like I want you to."

I approached the alley entrance. "I'm going in, boy. You follow me."

"I don't dig you, daddy."

"You follow me, boy, 'cause I'm just aching to feed you a fistful of brass knucks right in that big mouth of yours." I fairly shouted the last words.

I stepped into the alley and pressed against the wall, sick with fright. The stench of garbage and urine surrounded me. High above the buildings' black silhouette stars shone in a clear sky. I listened for his footsteps, ready to bolt if he accepted the challenge.

"Blessed St. Jude," I heard myself whisper, "send the bastard away," and I wondered from what source within me the prayer had spontaneously sprung.

After what seemed a long time, I stuck my head around the alley corner and looked back along the street. It stretched empty to the street lamp at the end.

I hurried to Dryades and along it to the well-lighted steps of the Catholic church I had visited in the afternoon. Sitting on the bottom step, I rested my head on my crossed arms and waited for my nerves to settle to calm. A great bell from the tower slowly rolled eight o'clock. I listened as the metallic clangor rolled away over the rooftops of the quarter.

The word "nigger" picked up the bell's resonances and repeated itself again and again in my brain.

Hey, nigger, you can't go in there.

Hey, nigger, you can't drink here.

We don't serve niggers.

And then the boy's words: *Mr. No-Hair, Daddy, Shithead.* (Would it have happened if I were white?)

And then the doctor's words as I left his office yesterday: *Now you go into oblivion.*

Seated on the church steps tonight, I wondered if he could have known how truly he spoke, how total the feeling of oblivion was.

A police car cruised past, slowed. The plaster-white face of an officer peered toward me. We stared at one another as the car took a right turn and disappeared behind the decrepit rectory of the church. I felt certain the police would circle the block and check on me. The cement was suddenly hard to my seat. I rose and hurried toward a little Negro café in the next block.

As I stepped through the door, the Negro woman sang out: "All we got left's beans and rice, honey."

"That's fine. Bring me a big plate," I said, sinking into a chair.

"How about some beer?"

"No . . . you got any milk?"

"Don't you like beer, honey?"

"I like it, but I've got diabetes."

"Oh. . . . Say, I've got a couple of pig tails left. You want me to put them in with the beans?"

"Please."

She carried the platter to my table and fetched my milk. Though Negroes apparently live on beans and rice in this area, it is no handicap. They are delicious and nourishing. I tried to eat the pig tails, but like chicken necks, they are mostly bone and little meat.

Later, in my room, I undressed for bed. The game still went noisily at the Y next door. Though the large house was still, I heard the TV from Mrs. Davis's room somewhere on the other side.

The whites seemed far away, out there in their parts of the city. The distance between them and me was far more than the miles that physically separated us. It was an area of unknowing. I wondered if it could really be bridged.

▼ ▼ ▼

Two days of incessant walking, mostly looking for jobs. I wanted to discover what sort of work an educated Negro, nicely dressed, could find. I met no rebuffs, only gentleness when they informed me they could not use my services as typist, bookkeeper, etc.

The patterns became the same. Each day at the shine stand we had the same kind of customers; each day we cooked food and ate on the sidewalk; each day we fed the beggar and the pigeons.

The widow woman dropped by both days. I gently let her know that I was married. Sterling said she asked him about me, proposing to invite me to her house for Sunday dinner. I stayed at the stand less and less.

Among Negroes I was treated with the most incredible courtesies, even by strangers.

One night I decided to go to a Negro movie house. I walked up Dryades and asked a young boy if he could tell me the way.

"If you'll wait just a minute, I'll show you the way," he said.

I stood on the corner and in a moment he returned.

We began walking. He was a first-year student at Dillard University, hoping to become a sociologist, to "do something for our people." The walk appeared to be endless. We must have gone at least two miles when I asked: "Do you live over in this direction?"

"No, I live back there where you saw me."

"But this is taking you way out of your way."

"I don't mind. I enjoy the talk."

When we reached the movie, he asked, "Do you think you can find the way back?"

"Oh, yes . . . I won't have any trouble."

"If you aren't sure, I can find out what time the feature ends and come back for you."

41

Stupefied that he would walk these miles as a courtesy to a stranger, I suggested he let me buy him a ticket for the show and we could walk back together.

"No, thanks—I have to get some studying done. But I'll be glad to come back for you."

"I wouldn't think of it. At least let me pay you something. This has been a great favor."

He refused the money.

The next morning I went to the Y café next door for breakfast of grits and eggs. The elderly gentleman who ran the café soon had me talking—or rather listening. He foresaw a new day for the race. Great strides had been made, but greater ones were to be made still. I told him of my unsuccessful job-hunting. He said it was all part of the pattern of economics—economic injustice.

"You take a young white boy. He can go through school and college with a real incentive. He knows he can make good money in any profession when he gets out. But can a Negro—in the South? No, I've seen many make brilliant grades in college. And yet when they come home in the summers to earn a little money, they have to do the most menial work. And even when they graduate it's a long hard pull. Most take postal jobs, or preaching or teaching jobs. *This is the cream.* What about the others, Mr. Griffin? A man knows no matter how hard he works, he's never going to *quite* manage . . . taxes and prices eat up more than he can earn. He can't see how he'll ever have a wife and children. The economic structure just doesn't permit it unless he's prepared to live down in poverty and have his wife work too. That's part of it. Our people aren't educated because they either can't afford it or else they know education won't earn them the jobs it would a white man. Any kind of family life, any decent standard of living seems impossible from the outset. So a lot of them, without even understanding the cause, just give up. They take what they can—mostly in pleasure, and they make the grand gesture, the wild gesture, because what have they got to lose if they do die in a car wreck or a knife fight or something else equally stupid."

"Yes, and then it's these things that cause the whites to say we're not worthy of first-class citizenship."

"Ah. . . ." he dropped his hands to his sides hard in frustration. "Isn't it so? They make it impossible for us to earn, to pay much in taxes because we haven't much in income, and then they say that because they pay most of the taxes, they have the right to have things like they want. It's a vicious circle, Mr. Griffin, and I don't know how we'll get out of it. They put us low, and then blame us for being down there and say that since we are low, we can't deserve our rights."

Others entered, ordered breakfast and joined the conversation.

"Equal job opportunities," Mr. Gayle said. "That's the answer to much of the tragedy of our young people."

"What's needed?" I asked. "What kind of wisdom can overcome the immense propaganda of the racists and the hate groups? People read this poison—and it's often presented in a benevolent tone, even a kind tone. Many sincerely think the Negro, because of his very Negro-ness, could not possibly measure up to white standards in work performance. I read recently where one of them said that equality of education and job opportunity would be an even greater tragedy for us. He said it would quickly prove to us that we can't measure up—disillusion us by showing us that we are, in fact, inferior."

"I wish those kind souls wouldn't be so protective. I know plenty who'd be willing to take the chance of being 'disillusioned,' " the proprietor laughed.

"They're about fifty years behind the times," an elderly man said. "The social scientists have shown this is wrong. Our own people have proven themselves in every field—not just a few, but thousands. How can the racists deny these proofs?"

"They don't bother to find out about them," Mr. Gayle said flatly.

"We need a conversion of morals," the elderly man said. "Not just superficially, but profoundly. And in both races. We need a great saint—some enlightened common sense. Otherwise, we'll never have the right answers when these pressure groups—those racists, superpatriots, whatever you want to call them—tag every move toward racial justice as communist-inspired, Zionist-inspired, Illuminati-inspired, Satan-inspired . . . part of some secret conspiracy to overthrow the Christian civilization."

"So, if you want to be a good Christian, you mustn't act like one. That makes sense," Mr. Gayle said.

"That's what they claim. The minute you give me my rights to vote when I pay taxes, to have a decent job, a decent home, a decent education—then you're taking that first step toward 'race-mixing' and that's part of the great secret conspiracy to ruin civilization—to ruin America."

"So, if you want to be a good American, you've got to practice bad Americanism. That makes sense, too," Mr. Gayle sighed. "Maybe it'd take a saint after all to straighten such a mess out."

"We've reached a poor state when people are afraid that doing the decent and right thing is going to help the communist conspiracy," the proprietor said. "I'm sure a lot of people are held back just on that point."

"Any way you look at it, we're in the middle. It's hard for me to understand how letting me have a decent job, so I can raise my children in a better home and give them a better education is going to help the enemies of my country. . . ."

Walking along Dryades, through the ghetto, I realized that every informed man with whom I had spoken, in the intimate freedom of the colored bond, had acknowledged a double problem for the Negro. First, the discrimination against him. Second, and almost more grievous, his discrimination against himself; his contempt for the blackness that he associates with his suffering; his willingness to sabotage his fellow Negroes because they are part of the blackness he has found so painful.

"Want something, mister?" a white merchant said as I passed. I glanced at him sitting in the doorway of his junky store. "Come on in," he wheedled, sounding for the world as though he were pimping for the shoes he had on display.

I had not gone ten feet when I heard him solicit someone else in the same tone. "Want something, mister?"

"Yeah, but you ain't my type," the man behind me answered without humor.

On Chartres Street in the French Quarter I walked toward Brennan's, one of New Orleans' famed restaurants. Forgetting myself for a moment, I stopped to study the menu that was elegantly exposed in a show window. I read, realizing that a few days earlier I could have gone in and ordered anything on the menu. But now, though I was the same person with the same appetite, the same appreciation and even the same wallet, no power on earth could get me inside this place for a meal. I recalled hearing some Negro say, "You can live here all your life, but you'll never get inside one of the great restaurants except as kitchen boy." The Negro often dreams of things separated from him only by a door, knowing that he is forever cut off from experiencing them.

I read the menu carefully, forgetting that Negroes do not do such things. It is too poignant, like the little boy peering in the candy store window. It might affect the tourist.

I looked up to see the frowns of disapproval that can speak so plainly and so loudly without words. The Negro learns this silent language fluently. He knows by the white man's look of disapproval and petulance that he is being told to get on his way, that he is "stepping out of line."

It was a day of giving the gracious smile and receiving the gracious rebuff as I asked again and again about jobs.

Finally, I gave up and went to the shine stand. From there I set out to return at dusk to Dryades. But I had walked too far. My legs gave out. At Jackson Square, a public park, I found a long, curving bench and sat down to rest for a moment. The park appeared deserted. A movement through the bushes attracted my attention. I looked to see a middle-aged white man across the park slowly fold the newspaper he was reading, get to his feet and amble toward me. The fragrance of his pipe tobacco preceded him, reassuring me. Racists are not the pipe-smoking type, I thought to myself.

With perfect courtesy he said, "You'd better find yourself someplace else to rest."

I took it as a favor. He was warning me so I could get

out before someone insulted me. "Thank you," I said. "I didn't know we weren't allowed in here."

Later, I told the story at the Y, and discovered that Negroes have the right to sit in Jackson Square. This individual simply did not want me there.

But at the time I did not know it. I left, sick with exhaustion, wondering where a Negro could sit to rest. It was walk constantly until you could catch a bus, but keep on the move unless you have business somewhere. If you stop to sit on the curb, a police car will pass and probably ask you what you're doing. I have heard none of the Negroes speak of police harassment, but they have warned me that any time the police see a Negro idling, especially one they do not recognize, they will surely question him. This is worrisome, certainly an experience any Negro wants to avoid.

I walked over to Claiborne and caught the first bus that passed. It took me out to Dillard University, a beautiful campus. I was too tired to explore it, however, and sat on the bench waiting to catch another bus into town. Buses were inexpensive to ride and it was a good way to rest.

Night was near when I finally caught the bus going toward town. Two blocks before Canal, the bus makes a left turn off Claiborne. I rang the bell to get off at this stop. The driver pulled to a halt and opened the door. He left it open until I reached it. I was ready to step off when the door banged shut in my face. Since he had to remain there waiting for a clear passage through traffic, I asked him to let me off.

"I can't leave the door open all night," he said impatiently.

He waited another full minute, but refused to open the door.

"Will you please let me off at the next corner, then?" I asked, controlling my temper, careful not to do or say anything that would jeopardize the Negroes' position in the area.

He did not answer. I returned to my seat. A woman watched me with sympathetic anger, as though she in no way approved of this kind of treatment. However, she did not speak.

At each stop, I sounded the buzzer, but the driver continued through the next two stops. He drove me eight full blocks past my original stop and pulled up then only because some white passengers wanted to get off. I followed them to the front. He watched me, his hand on the lever that would spring the doors shut.

"May I get off now?" I asked quietly when the others had stepped down.

"Yeah, go ahead," he said finally, as though he had tired of the cat-and-mouse game. I got off, sick, wondering how I could ever walk those eight blocks back to my original stop.

In all fairness, I must add that this is the only example of deliberate cruelty I encountered on any of the city buses of New Orleans. Even though I was outraged, I knew he did not commit this indignity against me, but against my black flesh, my color. This was an individual act by an individual, and certainly not typical.

▼ ▼ ▼

NOVEMBER 14

After a week of wearying rejection, the newness had worn off. My first vague, favorable impression that it was not as bad as I had thought it would be came from courtesies of the whites toward the Negro in New Orleans. But this was superficial. All the courtesies in the world do not cover up the one vital and massive discourtesy—that the Negro is treated not even as a second-class citizen, but as a tenth-class one. His day-to-day living is a reminder of his inferior status. He does not become calloused to these things—the polite rebuffs when he seeks better employment; hearing himself referred to as nigger, coon, jigaboo; having to bypass available rest-room facilities or eating facilities to find one specified for him. Each new reminder strikes at the raw spot, deepens the wound. I do not speak here only from my personal reaction, but from seeing it happen to others, and from seeing their reactions.

The Negro's only salvation from complete despair lies in his belief, the old belief of his forefathers, that these things are not directed against him personally, but against his race, his pigmentation. His mother or aunt or teacher long ago carefully prepared him, explaining that he as an individual can live in dignity, even though he as a Negro cannot. "They don't do it to you because you're Johnny—they don't even know you. They do it against your Negro-ness."

But at the time of the rebuff, even when the rebuff is impersonal, such as holding his bladder until he can find a "Colored" sign, the Negro cannot rationalize. He feels it personally and it burns him. It gives him a view of the white man that the white can never understand; for if the Negro is part of the black mass, the white is always the individual, and he will sincerely deny that he is "like that," he has always tried to be fair and kind to the Negro. Such men are offended to find Negroes suspicious of them, never realizing that the Negro cannot understand how—since as individuals they are decent and "good" to the colored— the whites as a group can still contrive to arrange life so that it destroys the Negro's sense of personal value, degrades his human dignity, deadens the fibers of his being.

Existence becomes a grinding effort, guided by belly-hunger and the almost desperate need to divert awareness from the squalors to the pleasures, to lose oneself in sex or drink or dope or gut-religion or gluttony or the incoherence of falsity; and in some instances in the higher pleasures of music, art, literature, though these usually deepen perceptions rather than dull them, and can be unbearable; they present a world that is ordered, sane, disciplined to felicity, and the contrast of that world to theirs increases the pain of theirs.

When I went out that morning the face of the Negro populace was glum and angry.

At the shoe stand, Sterling did not give his usual cordial greeting. His eyes looked yellower than usual.

"You heard?" he asked.

"No . . . I haven't heard anything . . ."

He told me the Mississippi jury refused to indict in the Parker lynch case. The news had spread over the quarter like a wave of acid. Everyone talked of it. Not since I was in Europe, when the Russo-German Pact of 1939 was signed, had I seen news spread such bitterness and despair.

Sterling handed me this morning's issue of *The Louisiana Weekly,* a Negro newspaper. The editorial page condemned the jury's actions.

If there was any doubt as to how "Southern Justice" operates in the State of Mississippi, it was completely dispelled . . . when the Pearl River County Grand Jury failed to return any indictments or even consider the massive information compiled by the FBI in the sensational Mack Parker kidnap-lynch murder case. . . . The axiom that a man is innocent until proved guilty by a court of law has been flagrantly ignored once again in the State of Mississippi. The fact that an accused man was deprived of a fair trial, kidnapped and murdered by a lynch mob from a Mississippi jail apparently had no effect on the thinking of the Grand Jury. The silent treatment merely gave approval of the mob taking the law into its hands. Mississippi has long had a reputation of failing to punish white men accused of criminal acts against Negroes. This is Mississippi's peculiar way of making Negroes "happy and contented" with the democratic processes and of showing the world how well they care for the Negro in respecting his rights as an American citizen.

The point that crushed most was that the FBI had supplied a dossier of evidence identifying the lynchers, and the Pearl River County Grand Jury had decided not to look inside it.

I handed the paper back to Sterling. In a voice heavy with anger he held it at arm's length and read: "The calculated lack of respect for law and order in Mississippi has made it a veritable jungle of intimidation, terrorism and brutality where only the fittest survive. Further, it has shamed the United States in the eyes of the world and added to the shame of the South, already experiencing strained, tense and explosive race relations because white supremacy mob rule substitutes too often for democracy. . . ."

He lowered the paper. "That's what pisses me off. They

rant about how the rest of the country's against the Southern white—hell, how could they help being? Well, this just proves it. This is what we can expect from the white man's justice. What hope is there when a white jury won't even *look* at the evidence against the lynch mob?"

I could find nothing to say.

"We might as well learn not to expect *nothing* from Southern Justice. They're going to stack the cards against us every time," Sterling said.

No one outside of the Negro community could imagine the profound effect this action had in killing the Negro's hope and breaking his morale.

I decided it was time to go into that state so dreaded by Negroes.

Joe returned with peanuts to sell. I told them of my decision to move into Mississippi.

They jumped on the news almost angrily. "What the hell you want to go there for?" Joe protested. "That's no place for a colored man—especially now with this Parker mess."

"They're going to treat any Negro like a dog," Sterling said. "You sure better not go."

"That's part of my work."

"I'm telling you," Joe insisted. "I know. I been there once and I couldn't get out quick enough. And things weren't as bad then as they are now."

"Yes, but Mississippi tells the rest of the world they got a wonderful relationship with their Negroes—that they understand each other, and like each other. They say outsiders just don't understand. Well, I'm going there to see if I can understand."

"It's your ass," Joe said. "But I sure hate to see you do it."

"You're going to come back and see us sometime, aren't you?" Sterling said.

"You bet," I said, walking away. A clumsy good-by.

My money was running low so I decided to cash some travelers checks before leaving. The banks were closed, since it was past noon on Saturday, but I felt I would have no difficulty with travelers checks in any of the larger stores, especially those on Dryades where I had traded and was known as a customer.

I took the bus to Dryades and walked down it, stopping at the dime store where I'd made most of my purchases. The young white girl came forward to wait on me.

"I need to cash a travelers check," I said smiling.

"We don't cash any checks of any kind," she said firmly.

"But a travelers check is perfectly safe," I said.

"We just don't cash checks," she said and turned away.

"Look, you know me. You've waited on me. I need some money."

"You should have gone to the bank."

"I didn't know I needed the money until after the banks closed," I said.

I knew I was making a pest of myself, but I could scarcely believe this nice young lady could be so unsympathetic, so insolent when she discovered I did not come in to buy something.

"I'll be glad to buy a few things," I said.

She called up to the bookkeeping department on an open mezzanine. "Hey! Do we cash travelers ch——"

"No!" the white woman shouted back.

"Thank you for your kindness," I said and walked out.

I went into one store after the other along Dryades and Rampart Streets. In every store their smiles turned to grimaces when they saw I meant not to buy but to cash a check. It was not their refusal—I could understand that; it was the bad manners they displayed. I began to feel desperate and resentful. They would have cashed a travelers check without hesitation for a white man. Each time they refused me, they implied clearly that I had probably come by these checks dishonestly and they wanted nothing to do with them or me.

Finally, after I gave up hope and decided I must remain in New Orleans without funds until the banks opened on Monday, I walked toward town. Small gold-lettering on the window of a store caught my attention: CATHOLIC BOOK STORE. Knowing the Catholic stand on racism, I wondered if this shop might cash a Negro's check. With some hesitation, I opened the door and entered. I was prepared to be disappointed.

"Would you cash a twenty-dollar travelers check for me?" I asked the proprietress.

"Of course," she said without hesitation, as though nothing could be more natural. She did not even study me.

I was so grateful I bought a number of paperback books—works of Maritain, Aquinas and Christopher Dawson. With these in my jacket, I hurried toward the Greyhound bus station.

In the bus station lobby, I looked for signs indicating a colored waiting room, but saw none. I walked up to the ticket counter. When the lady ticket-seller saw me, her otherwise attractive face turned sour, violently so. This look was so unexpected and so unprovoked I was taken aback.

"What do you want?" she snapped.

Taking care to pitch my voice to politeness, I asked about the next bus to Hattiesburg.

She answered rudely and glared at me with such loathing I knew I was receiving what the Negroes call "the hate stare." It was my first experience with it. It is far more than the look of disapproval one occasionally gets. This was so exaggeratedly hateful I would have been amused if I had not been so surprised.

I framed the words in my mind: "Pardon me, but have I done something to offend you?" But I realized I had done nothing—my color offended her.

"I'd like a one-way ticket to Hattiesburg, please," I said and placed a ten-dollar bill on the counter.

"I can't change that big a bill," she said abruptly and turned away, as though the matter were closed. I remained at the window, feeling strangely abandoned but not knowing what else to do. In a while she flew back at me, her face flushed, and fairly shouted: "I *told* you—I can't change that big a bill."

"Surely," I said stiffly, "in the entire Greyhound system there must be some means of changing a ten-dollar bill. Perhaps the manager—"

She jerked the bill furiously from my hand and stepped

away from the window. In a moment she reappeared to hurl my change and the ticket on the counter with such force most of it fell on the floor at my feet. I was truly dumfounded by this deep fury that possessed her whenever she looked at me. Her performance was so venomous, I felt sorry for her. It must have shown in my expression, for her face congested to high pink. She undoubtedly considered it a supreme insolence for a Negro to dare to feel sorry for her.

I stooped to pick up my change and ticket from the floor. I wondered how she would feel if she learned that the Negro before whom she had behaved in such an unladylike manner was habitually a white man.

With almost an hour before bus departure, I turned away and looked for a place to sit. The large, handsome room was almost empty. No other Negro was there, and I dared not take a seat unless I saw some other Negro also seated.

Once again a "hate stare" drew my attention like a magnet. It came from a middle-aged, heavy-set, well-dressed white man. He sat a few yards away, fixing his eyes on me. Nothing can describe the withering horror of this. You feel lost, sick at heart before such unmasked hatred, not so much because it threatens you as because it shows humans in such an inhuman light. You see a kind of insanity, something so obscene the very obscenity of it (rather than its threat) terrifies you. It was so new I could not take my eyes from the man's face. I felt like saying: "What in God's name are you doing to yourself?"

A Negro porter sidled over to me. I glimpsed his white coat and turned to him. His glance met mine and communicated the sorrow, the understanding.

"Where am I supposed to go?" I asked him.

He touched my arm in that mute and reassuring way of men who share a moment of crisis. "Go outside and around the corner of the building. You'll find the room."

The white man continued to stare, his mouth twisted with loathing as he turned his head to watch me move away.

In the colored waiting room, which was not labeled as such, but rather as COLORED CAFÉ, presumably because of interstate travel regulations, I took the last empty seat. The room was crowded with glum faces, faces dead to all enthusiasm, faces of people waiting.

The books I had bought from the Catholic Book Store weighed heavily in my pocket. I pulled one of them out and, without looking at the title, let it fall open in my lap. I read:

"... *it is by justice that we can authentically measure man's value or his nullity* ... *the absence of justice is the absence of what makes him man.*" Plato.

I have heard it said another way, as a dictum: "*He who is less than just is less than man.*"

I copied the passage in a little pocket notebook. A Negro woman, her face expressionless, flat, highlighted with sweat, watched me write. When I turned in my seat to put the notebook in my hip pocket, I detected the faintest smile at the corners of her mouth.

They called the bus. We filed out into the high-roofed garage and stood in line, the Negroes to the rear, the whites to the front. Buses idled their motors, filling the air with a stifling odor of exhaust fumes. An army officer hurried to get at the rear of the white line. I stepped back to let him get in front. He refused and went to the end of the colored portion of the line. Every Negro craned his head to look at the phenomenon. I have learned that men in uniform, particularly officers, rarely descend to show discrimination, perhaps because of the integration of the armed forces.

We sweated through our clothes and I was ready to leave and try for a later bus when they allowed us to board. Though nominally segregation is not permitted on interstate buses, no Negro would be fool enough to try to sit anywhere except at the rear on one going into Mississippi. I occupied a seat to myself not far from the back. Muffled conversations sprang up around me.

"Well, here we go into Mississippi—the most lied-about state in the union—that's what they claim," a man behind me said.

"It's the truth, too," another said. "Only it's Mississippi that does all the lying."

We drove through New Orleans under an overcast sky.

Air conditioning in the bus cooled us comfortably. As we crossed the bridge, the water of Lake Pontchartrain reflected the sky's gray tone, with whitecaps on its disturbed surface.

The bus stopped at the outskirts of town to take on more passengers. Among them was a striking Negro man, tall, slender, elegantly dressed—the "Valentino" type. He wore a mustache and a neatly trimmed Van Dyke beard. He walked toward the rear, giving the whites a fawning, almost tender look. His expression twisted to a sneer when he reached the back and surveyed the Negroes.

He sat sidewise in an empty seat across the aisle from me and began to harangue two brothers behind him. "This place stinks. Damned punk niggers. Look at all of them—bunch of dirty punks—don't know how to dress. You don't deserve anything better. *Mein Kampf!* Do you speak German? No. You're ignorant. You make me sick."

He proceeded to denounce his race venomously. He spoke fragments of French, Spanish and Japanese.

I averted my head to the window and watched the country fly past as we traveled through an area of sunlight. I did not want to become involved in any discussion with this strange man. He was soon in violent argument with one of the brothers. They quarreled to the point of rage over whether Juárez was in Old Mexico or New Mexico.

The elegant one shouted, "You can't lie to Christophe. Christophe's got brains. No ignorant punk like you can fool him. You never been to Juárez!"

He jumped abruptly to his feet. Fearing violence, I turned toward him. He stood poised, ready to strike the other, his eyes narrowed to slits of hatred.

"If you hit me, you'll just be hitting me in the wrong," the poorly dressed Negro said, looking calmly up at Christophe. His seat companion added with a gentle smile, "He's my brother. I'd have to take his part."

"You threatening me?" Christophe whispered.

"No, now look," the brother placated. "Why don't you two agree just not to talk."

"He won't say another word to me? You promise?" Christophe said. He lowered his fist, but his face did not relax.

"No, he won't—will you?"

The poorly dressed one shrugged his shoulders pleasantly. "I guess——"

"Don't speak! Don't speak!" Christophe shouted into his face.

"Okay . . . Okay . . ." he said, glancing toward me as though to say the elegant Christophe must be insane.

Christophe glared at him for some time before moving over into the seat next to me. His presence set my nerves on edge. He was cunning and apparently vicious and I did not know what kind of scene he might start. I stared out the window, turning so far he could see only the back of my head.

He slouched far down in the seat and, working his hands wildly in the air as though he were playing a guitar, he began to sing the blues, softly, mournfully, lowering his voice at the obscene words. A strange sweetish odor detached from him. I supposed it to be marijuana, but it was only a guess.

I felt his elbow dig into my ribs. "How you like that, pappy?"

I nodded, trying to be both polite and noncommittal. He had pulled his hat down over his eyes. He lighted a cigarette and let it dangle from his lips. I turned back to the window, hoping he would leave me alone.

He nudged me again and I looked around. He bent his head far back to gaze at me under his lowered hat brim. "You don't dig the blues, do you, daddy?"

"I don't know," I said.

He studied me with narrowed eyes. Then, as though he had found some answer, he flashed me a magnificent smile, leaned hard against me and whispered. "I bet you dig this, daddy."

He punched his hat back, concentrated, stiffened his hands, palms upward, in a supplicating gesture and began softly to chant *Tantun ergo sacramentum, Veneremur cernui* in as beautiful Latin as I have ever heard. I stared at him dumfounded as he chanted the Gregorian version of this famous text.

He glanced at me tenderly, his face soft as though he were on the verge of tears. "That got you, didn't it, dad?"

"Yes," I said.

He made a huge sign of the cross, lowered his head and recited, again with perfect Latin diction, the *Confiteor*. When it was over, he remained still, in profound introspection. Above the hum of the bus's wheels on the pavement, silence surrounded us. No one spoke. Doubtless those nearest us who had witnessed the strange scene were perplexed.

"You were an altar boy, I guess," I said.

"I was," he said, not raising his head. "I wanted to be a priest." His mobile face revealed every emotion. His eyes darkened with regret.

The man across the aisle grinned and said: "Better not believe anything he tells you."

Christophe's handsome face congealed instantly to hatred.

"I told you not to talk to me!"

The man's brother intervened. "He just forgot." Then to the poorly dressed one, "Don't say *anything* to him. He can't stand you."

"I was talking to the other fellow, the one in the dark glasses," he said.

"Shut up!" Christophe shouted. "You were talking *about* me—and I don't even want you to do that."

"Just be quiet," the man's brother said. "He's going to be mad at anything you say."

"Goddamn, it's a free sonofabitching country," the other said feebly, the smile remaining unchanged on his face. "I'm not afraid of him."

"Well, just hush—no need in you talking to him," his brother pleaded.

"You keep him quiet—or else," Christophe said haughtily.

My stomach contracted with uneasiness, certain there would be a fight. I was astonished to see Christophe cut his eyes around to me and wink, as though secretly he were amused. He glared his "enemy" down for some time before turning back to me. "I came to sit by you because you're the only one here that looks like he's got enough sense to carry on an intelligent conversation."

"Thank you," I said.

"I'm not pure Negro," he said proudly. "My mother was French, my father Indian."

"I see. . . ."

"She was Portuguese, my mother—a lovely woman," Christophe sighed.

"I see. . . ."

The man across the aisle smiled broadly at the obvious admission of a lie from Christophe. I gave him a warning glance and he did not challenge our friend's French-Portuguese-Indian background.

"Let's see," Christophe said, eying me speculatively. "What blood have you got? Give me a minute. Christophe never makes a mistake. I can always tell what kind of blood a man's got in him." He took my face between his hands and examined me closely. I waited, certain this strange man would expose me. Finally, he nodded gravely to indicate he had deciphered my blood background. "I have it now." His eyes glowed and he hesitated before making his dramatic announcement to the world. I cringed, preparing explanations, and then decided to try to stop him from exposing me.

"Wait—let me——"

"Florida Navaho," he interrupted triumphantly. "Your mother was part Florida Navaho, wasn't she?"

I felt like laughing, first with relief and then at the thought of my Dutch-Irish mother being anything so exotic as Florida Navaho. At the same time, I felt vaguely disappointed to find Christophe no brighter than the rest of us.

He waited for my answer.

"You're pretty sharp," I said.

"Ha! I never miss." Instantly, his expression degenerated to viciousness. "I hate us, Father."

"I'm not a Father."

"Ah, you can't fool Christophe. I know you're a priest even if you are dressed in civilian clothes. Look at these punks, Father. Dumb, ignorant bastards. They don't know the score. I'm getting out of this country."

His anger vanished. He leaned to whisper in my ear, his voice suddenly abject. "I'll tell you the truth, Father. I'm just out of the pen—four years. I'm on my way to see my wife. She's waiting with a new car for me in Slidell. And God . . . what a reunion we're going to have!"

His face crumpled and his head fell against my chest. Silently he wept.

"Don't cry," I whispered. "It's all right. Don't cry."

He raised his head and rolled his eyes upward in agony. His face bathed in tears, all of his arrogant defenses gone, he said: "Sometime, Father, when you say Mass, will you take the white Host for Christophe?"

"You're wrong to believe I'm a priest," I said. "But I'll remember you the next time I go to Mass."

"Ah, that's the only peace," he sighed. "That's the peace my soul longs for. I wish I could come back home to it, but I can't—I haven't been inside a church in seventeen years."

"You can always go back."

"Nah," he snorted. "I've got to shoot up a couple of guys."

My surprise must have shown. A smile of glee lighted his face. "Don't worry, daddy. I'm going to watch out. Why don't you get off with me and let's shoot up this town together."

I told him I could not. The bus slowed into Slidell. Christophe got to his feet, straightened his tie, stared furiously at the man across the aisle for a moment, bowed to me and got off. We were relieved to have him gone, though I could not help wondering what his life might be were he not torn with the frustrations of his Negro-ness.

At Slidell we changed into another Greyhound bus with a new driver—a middle-aged man, large-bellied with a heavy, jowled face filigreed with tiny red blood vessels near the surface of his cheeks.

A stockily built young Negro, who introduced himself as Bill Williams, asked if I minded having him sit beside me.

Now that Christophe was gone, the tensions disappeared in our Negro section. Everyone knew, from having heard our conversation, that I was a stranger in the area. Talk flowed easily and they surrounded me with warmth.

"People come down here and say Mississippi is the worst

place in the world," Bill said. "But we can't all live in the North."

"Of course not. And it looks like beautiful country," I said, glancing out at giant pine trees.

Seeing that I was friendly, he offered advice. "If you're not used to things in Mississippi, you'll have to watch yourself pretty close till you catch on," he said.

The others, hearing, nodded agreement.

I told him I did not know what to watch out for.

"Well, you know you don't want to even look at a white woman. In fact, you look down at the ground or the other way."

A large, pleasant Negro woman smiled at me across the aisle. "They're awful touchy on that here. You may not even know you're looking in a white woman's direction, but they'll try to make something out of it," she said.

"If you pass by a picture show, and they've got women on the posters outside, don't look at them either."

"Is it that bad?"

He assured me it was. Another man said: "Somebody's sure to say, 'Hey, boy—what are you looking at that white gal like *that* for?'"

I remembered the woman on the bus in New Orleans using almost the same expression.

"And you dress pretty well," Bill continued, his heavy black face frowning in concentration. "If you walk past an alley, walk out in the middle of the street. Plenty of people here, white and colored, would knock you in the head if they thought you had money on you. If white boys holler at you, just keep walking. Don't let them stop you and start asking you questions."

I told him I appreciated his warning.

"Can you all think of anything else?" he asked the others.

"That covers it," one of them said.

I thanked him for telling me these things.

"Well, if I was to come to your part of the country, I'd want somebody to tell me," Bill said.

He told me he was a truck driver, working out of Hattiesburg. He had taken a load to New Orleans, where he had left his truck for repairs and caught the bus back to Hattiesburg. He asked if I had made arrangements for a place to stay. I told him no. He said the best thing would be for me to contact a certain important person who would put me in touch with someone reliable who would find me a decent and safe place.

It was late dusk when the bus pulled into some little town for a stop. "We get about ten minutes here," Bill said. "Let's get off and stretch our legs. They've got a men's room here if you need to go."

The driver stood up and faced the passengers. "Ten-minute rest stop," he announced.

The whites rose and ambled off. Bill and I led the Ne-groes toward the door. As soon as he saw us, the driver blocked our way. Bill slipped under his arm and walked toward the dim-lit shed building.

"Hey, boy, where you going?" the driver shouted to Bill while he stretched his arms across the opening to prevent my stepping down. "Hey, you, boy, I'm talking to you." Bill's footsteps crunched unhurriedly across the gravel.

I stood on the bottom step, waiting. The driver turned back to me.

"Where do you think you're going?" he asked, his heavy cheeks quivering with each word.

"I'd like to go to the rest room." I smiled and moved to step down.

He tightened his grip on the door facings and shouldered in close to block me. "Does your ticket say for you to get off here?" he asked.

"No sir, but the others——"

"Then you get your ass back in your seat and don't you move till we get to Hattiesburg," he commanded.

"You mean I can't go to the——"

"I mean get your ass back there like I told you," he said, his voice rising. "I can't be bothered rounding up all you people when we get ready to go."

"You announced a rest stop. The whites all got off," I said, unable to believe he really meant to deprive us of rest-room privileges.

He stood on his toes and put his face up close to mine. His nose flared. Footlights caught silver glints from the hairs that curled out of his nostrils. He spoke slowly, threat-eningly: "Are you arguing with me?"

"No sir . . ." I sighed.

"Then you do like I say."

We turned like a small herd of cattle and drifted back to our seats. The others grumbled about how unfair it was. The large woman was apologetic, as though it embarrassed her for a stranger to see Mississippi's dirty linen.

"There's no call for him to act like that," she said. "They usually let us off."

I sat in the monochrome gloom of dusk, scarcely believing that in this year of freedom any man could deprive another of anything so basic as the need to quench thirst or use the rest room. There was nothing of the feel of America here. It was rather some strange country suspended in ugliness. Tension hung in the air, a continual threat, even though you could not put your finger on it.

"Well," I heard a man behind me say softly but firmly, "if I can't go in there, then I'm going in here. I'm not going to sit here and bust."

I glanced back and saw it was the same poorly dressed man who had so outraged Christophe. He walked in a half crouch to a place behind the last seat, where he urinated loudly on the floor. Indistinguishable sounds of approval rose around me—quiet laughter, clearing throats, whispers.

"Let's all do it," a man said.

"Yeah, flood this bus and end all this damned foolishness."

Bitterness dissolved in our delight to give the bus driver and the bus as good as they deserved.

The move was on, but it was quelled by another voice: "No, let's don't. It'll just give them something else to hold against us," an older man said. A woman agreed. All of us could see the picture. The whites would start claiming that we were unfit, that Negroes did not even know enough to go to the rest room—they just did it in the back of the bus; never mentioning, of course, that the driver would not let us off.

The driver's bullish voice attracted our attention.

"Didn't you hear me call you?" he asked as Bill climbed the steps.

"I sure didn't," Bill said pleasantly.

"You deaf?"

"No sir."

"You mean to stand there and say you didn't hear me call you?"

"Oh, were you calling me?" Bill asked innocently. "I heard you yelling 'Boy,' but that's not my name, so I didn't know you meant me."

Bill returned and sat beside me, surrounded by the approval of his people. In the immense tug-of-war, such an act of defiance turned him into a hero.

As we drove more deeply into Mississippi, I noted that the Negro comforted and sought comfort from his own. Whereas in New Orleans he paid little attention to his brother, in Mississippi everyone who boarded the bus at the various little towns had a smile and a greeting for everyone else. We felt strongly the need to establish friendship as a buffer against the invisible threat. Like shipwrecked people, we huddled together in a warmth and courtesy that was pure and pathetic.

The threat grew as we penetrated deeper toward the center of the state. The distance between the whites and the blacks grew tangibly greater, even though we saw only the backs of their heads and shoulders, their hats and the cigarette smoke rising from them as night fell and bus lights switched on. They said nothing, did not look back, but hostility emanated from them in an unmistakable manner.

We tried to counter it by being warm and kind to one another, far more than strangers usually are. Women discussed where they lived and promised to visit one another, though all knew that such visits would never take place.

As we neared Poplarville, agitation swept through the bus. Everyone's mind was on the Parker youth's lynching and the jury's refusal to consider the FBI evidence against his lynchers.

"Do you know about Poplarville?" Bill whispered.

"Yes."

Some of the whites looked back. Animated Negro faces turned stony.

Bill pointed out places in a quiet expressionless voice. "That's the jail where they snatched him. They went up to his cell—the bastards—and grabbed his feet and dragged

him down so his head bumped against each stairstep. They
found blood on them, and blood at the bottom landing. He
must've known what they were going to do to him. He
must've been scared shitless."

The bus circled through the streets of a small Southern
town, a gracious town in appearance. I looked about me. It
was too real for my companions, too vivid. Their faces were
pinched, their expressions indrawn as though they felt
themselves being dragged down the jail stairway, felt their
own heads bumping against the steps, experiencing the
terror . . .

Bill's voice cut through, sourly: "That's the courthouse
where they made that decision." He looked at me to see
if I understood what decision he meant. I nodded.

"That's where they as much as told the whites, 'You go
ahead and lynch those niggers, we'll see you don't get in any
trouble.' "

I wondered what the whites in front were thinking. The
lynching and the callous decision of the Pearl River County
Grand Jury were surely on all their minds. Perhaps the
injustice was as nightmarish to them as it was to those surrounding me.

We drove through wooded countryside into the night.
Bill dozed beside me, his snores adjusted to the hum of the
tires. No one talked. After a while Bill roused himself and
pointed out the window. "That's where they fished his body
out of the creek," he said. I cupped my hands to the window but could see only black masses of foliage against a
dark sky.

We arrived at Hattiesburg around eight thirty. Most of
the Negroes hurried to the rest rooms. Bill gave me instructions with such solicitude that I was alarmed. Why,
unless there was real danger, would he be so careful to help
me avoid it? I wondered. He told me where I should go
first, and whom I should request to see.

"What's the best way to get there?" I asked.

"Have you got some money?"

"Yes."

"Take a cab."

"Where do I catch one?"

"Any of those cabs out there," he said pointing to a string of parked cabs driven by white men.

"You mean a white driver'll take a Negro passenger?" I asked.

"Yeah."

"They wouldn't in New Orleans . . . they said they weren't allowed to."

"They're allowed to do anything to get your dime here," he said. We walked to one of the cabs.

"Yessir, where can I take you?" the driver said. I looked through the window to see a pleasant young man who showed no hint of animosity. Bill told him the address where he should deliver me.

"Wait just a second, will you?" Bill told the driver. He grabbed my arm and walked away.

"I'll find out where you're staying. I'll come around about noon tomorrow and check on you to see you're all right."

Again I was overwhelmed that strangers should go to such trouble for me.

I thanked him. He hesitated, as though uncertain and then said. "I'm not buttin' into your business, but if you're planning on getting a girl—you don't want to get one that'll burn you."

"I sure don't." I thought of La Fontaine's *Les deux amis,* where the friend offers to help rid the hero of his sadness, even to procuring a girl for him. I detected no hint of lasciviousness in Bill's voice or manner, certainly no element of pimping; no, he was simply trying to protect me.

"If you do plan on getting one, you better let me help you find a clean one."

"I'm worn out, Bill," I said. "I guess I'll bypass it tonight."

"That's fine . . . I just didn't want you to go getting yourself messed up."

"I appreciate it."

The cab driver delivered me to an address on Mobile Street, the main street of the Negro quarter. It was narrow, cluttered, lined by stores, cafés, bars. He was completely civil, and in such an authentic way, I felt it was his real nature and not just a veneer to please the customer—the way I had seen it in the stores in New Orleans.

"Looks awful wild down here," I said as I paid him. I had to speak loudly to make him hear me above the shouts and the amplified wails of juke-box rock-and-roll music.

"If you don't know the quarter, you'd better get inside somewhere as soon as you can," he said.

My contact inside referred me to another person in the quarter. As I walked down Mobile Street, a car full of white men and boys sped past. They yelled obscenities at me. A satsuma (tangerine) flew past my head and broke against a building. The street was loud and raw, with tension as thick as fog.

I felt the insane terror of it. When I entered the store of my second contact, we talked in low voices, though he made no effort to be guarded or cautious in expressing his contempt for the brutes who made forays into the area.

"The sonsabitches beat one boy to a pulp. He was alone on a stretch of walk. They jumped out of the car, tore him up and were gone before anyone knew what was happening," he said. "They framed another on a trumped-up charge of carrying whisky in his car. He's one of the finest boys in town. Never drinks."

His bitterness was so great I knew I would be thought a spy for the whites if I divulged my identity.

Another car roared down the street, and the street was suddenly deserted, but the Negroes appeared again shortly. I sought refuge in a Negro drugstore and drank milk shakes as an excuse to stay there.

A well-dressed man approached and asked if I were Mr. Griffin. I told him I was. He said there was a room for me and I could go to it whenever I got ready.

I walked through the street again, through the darkness that was alive with lights and humanity. Blues boomed from a tavern across the street. It was a sort of infernal circus, smelling of barbecue and kerosene.

My room was upstairs in a wooden shanty structure that had never known paint. It was decrepit, but the Negro leaders assured me it was safe and that they would keep a close watch on me. Without turning on my light, I went over and sat on the bed. Lights from the street cast a yellowish glow over the room.

From the tavern below a man improvised a ballad about "poor Mack Parker . . . overcome with passion . . . his body in the creek."

"Oh Lord," a woman said in the quiet that followed, her voice full of sadness and awe.

"Lordy . . . Lordy . . ." a man said in a hushed voice, as though there were nothing more he could say.

Canned jazz blared through the street with a monstrous high-strutting rhythm that pulled at the viscera. The board floor squeaked under my footsteps. I switched on the light and looked into a cracked piece of mirror bradded with bent nails to the wall. The bald Negro stared back at me from its mottled sheen. I knew I was in hell. Hell could be no more lonely or hopeless, no more agonizingly estranged from the world of order and harmony.

I heard my voice, as though it belonged to someone else, hollow in the empty room, detached, say: "Nigger, what you standing up there crying for?"

I saw tears slick on his cheeks in the yellow light.

Then I heard myself say what I have heard them say so many times. "It's not right. It's just not right."

Then the onrush of revulsion, the momentary flash of blind hatred against the whites who were somehow responsible for all of this, the old bewilderment of wondering, "Why do they do it? Why do they keep us like this? What are they gaining? What evil has taken them?" (The Negroes say, "What sickness has taken them?") My revulsion turned to grief that my own people could give the hate stare, could shrivel men's souls, could deprive humans of rights they unhesitatingly accord their livestock.

I turned away from the mirror. A burned-out light globe lay on the plank floor in the corner. Its unfrosted glass held the reflection of the overhead bulb, a speck of brightness. A half-dozen film negatives curled up around it like dead leaves. I picked them up and held them before the light with strange excitement, curious to see the image that some prior occupant of this room had photographed.

Each negative was blank.

I imagined him going to the drugstore to pick up the

package of photos and hurrying to this squalid room to warm himself with the view of his wife, his children, his parents, his girl friend—who knows? He had sat here holding blank negatives, masterpieces of human ingenuity wasted.

I flicked the negatives, as he must have done, toward the corner, heard them scratch dryly against the wall and flap to the floor. One struck the dead globe, causing it to sing its strange filamental music of the spheres, fragile and high-pitched above the outside noises.

Music from the juke box, a grinding rhythm, ricocheted down the street.

                        hangity
            hangity   *hangity*   *oomp*
    Harangity   *oomp*   *oomp*

The aroma of barbecue tormented my empty insides, but I did not want to leave the room to go back into the mainstream of hell.

I took out my notebook, lay across the bed on my stomach and attempted to write—anything to escape the death dance out there in the Mississippi night. But the intimate contentment would not come. I tried to write my wife —I needed to write to her, to give her my news—but I found I could tell her nothing. No words would come. She had nothing to do with this life, nothing to do with the room in Hattiesburg or with its Negro inhabitant. It was maddening. All my instincts struggled against the estrangement. I began to understand Lionel Trilling's remark that culture—learned behavior patterns so deeply engrained they produce unconscious, involuntary reactions—is a prison. My conditioning as a Negro, and the immense sexual implications with which the racists in our culture bombard us, cut me off, even in my most intimate self, from any connection with my wife.

I stared at the letter and saw written: *Hattiesburg, November 14. My darling,* followed by a blank page.

The visual barrier imposed itself. The observing self saw the Negro, surrounded by the sounds and smells of the ghetto, write "Darling" to a white woman. The chains of my blackness would not allow me to go on. Though I understood and could analyze what was happening, I could not break through.

Never look at a white woman—look down or the other way.

What do you mean, calling a white woman "darling" like that, boy?

I went out to find some barbecue, down the outside steps, my hand on the cool weathered railing, past a man leaning forward with his head cushioned on his arm against a wall, leaking into the shadows; and on into a door somewhere. There were dim lights and signs: NO OBSENETY ALLOWED and HOT LINKS 25¢.

A round-faced woman, her cheeks slicked yellow with sweat, handed me a barbecued beef sandwich. My black hands took it from her black hands. The imprint of her thumb remained in the bread's soft pores. Standing so close, odors of her body rose up to me from her white uniform, a mingling of hickory-smoked flesh, gardenia talcum and sweat. The expression on her full face cut into me. Her eyes said with unmistakable clarity, "God . . . isn't it awful?" She took the money and stepped back into the open kitchen. I watched her lift the giant lid of the pit and fork out a great chunk of meat. White smoke billowed up, hazing her face to gray.

The meat warmed through the bread in my hand. I carried the sandwich outside and sat on the back steps leading up to my room to eat it. A streak of light from the front flowed past me, illuminating dusty weeds, debris and outbuildings some distance to the rear. The night, the hoots and shouts surrounded me even in this semihiding place.

hangity
hangity *hangity*
Harangity . . .

The music consumed in its blatant rhythm all other rhythms, even that of the heartbeat. I wondered how all of this would look to the casual observer, or to the whites in their homes. "The niggers are whooping it up over on Mobile Street tonight," they might say. "They're happy."

Or, as one scholar put it, "Despite their lowly status, they are capable of living jubilantly." Would they see the immense melancholy that hung over the quarter, so oppressive that men had to dull their sensibilities in noise or wine or sex or gluttony in order to escape it? The laughter had to be gross or it would turn to sobs, and to sob would be to realize, and to realize would be to despair. So the noise poured forth like a jazzed-up fugue, louder and louder to cover the whisper in every man's soul, "You are black. You are condemned." This is what the white man mistook for "jubilant living" and called "whooping it up." This is how the white man can say, "They live like dogs," never realizing why they must, to save themselves, shout, get drunk, shake the hip, pour pleasures into bellies deprived of happiness. Otherwise, the sounds from the quarter would lose order and rhythm and become wails.

I felt disaster. Somewhere in the night's future the tensions would explode into violence. The white boys would race through too fast. They would see a man or a boy or a woman alone somewhere along the street and the lust to beat or to kill would flood into them. Some frightful thing had to climax this accelerating madness.

Words of the state song hummed through my memory:

> *Way down South in Mississippi, Cotton blossoms white in the sun,*
> *We all love our Mississippi, Here we'll stay where livin' is fun.*
> *The evening stars shine brighter, And glad is every dewy morn,*
> *For way down South in Mississippi, Folks are happy they have been born.*

Scenes from books and movies came back—the laces, the shaded white-columned veranda with mint juleps served by an elegantly uniformed "darky," the honor, the magnolia fragrance, the cotton fields where "darkies, happy and contented," labored in the day and then gathered at the manse to serenade their beloved white folks with spirituals in the evening after supper . . . until the time when they could escape to freedom.

Here, tonight, it was the wood plank beneath my seat, the barbecue grease on my lips, the need to hide from white eyes degenerate with contempt . . . even in the land "where livin' is fun."

*And God is loved in Mississippi, Home and
church her people hold dear.*

I rose stiffly to my feet. Suddenly I knew I could not go back up to that room with its mottled mirror, its dead light bulb and its blank negatives.

I knew of one white man in Hattiesburg to whom I might turn for help—a newspaperman, P. D. East. But I hesitated to call him. He has been so persecuted for seeking justice in race relations I was afraid my presence anywhere near him might further jeopardize him.

I washed my hands and mouth under an outside faucet and walked around into the street to a phone.

P. D. was not at home, but I explained the situation to his wife, Billie. She said she was long ago inured to shocks, and insisted on having P. D. rescue me.

"Not if it's going to cause you people more trouble," I said. "I'm scared to death, but I'd rather stay here than get you in any deeper."

"It's late," she said. "I'll contact P. D. He can bring you here without your being seen. Stand in front of the drugstore. He'll pick you up. Only one thing. You're not to do any of your investigating around this area—okay?"

"Of course not," I said.

"I mean, that would really get us in a jam . . ."

"Of course—I wouldn't think of it."

I waited in front of the lighted drugstore which was closed down for the night. My nerves tightened each time a car passed. I expected another satsuma to be thrown or another oath to be hurled. Other Negroes stood in other doorways, watching me as though they thought I was insane to stand there in the bright light. A sensible man would wait in the darkness.

Moments later a station wagon passed slowly and parked a few yards down the street. I was certain it must be P. D. and wondered at his foolishness in parking where he would have to walk along a sidewalk toward me, past a gantlet of Negroes who might not recognize him and who had good cause that night to resent any white man.

He got out and walked easily toward me, huge in the dim light. I could not speak. He shook my Negro hand in full view of everyone on the street. Then in his soft and cultivated voice he said: "Are you ready to go?"

I nodded and we returned to his car. He held the door for me to get in and then drove off.

"It's amazing," he said, after an uncomfortable silence.

We drove through the darkened streets to his home, talking in a strangely stilted manner. I wondered why, and then realized that I had grown so accustomed to being a Negro, to being shown contempt, that I could not rid myself of the cautions. I was embarrassed to ride in the front seat of the car with a white man, especially on our way to his home. It was breaking the "Southern rule" somehow. Too, in this particular atmosphere my "escape" was an emotional thing felt by both of us.

I repeated my plea that he not take me home if it meant any embarrassment or danger for his wife and child. He ignored this.

When we drove into his carport, his wife stood in the shadows beside the house.

"Well, hello, Uncle Tom," she said.

Once again the terrible truth struck me. Here in America, in this day, the simple act of whites receiving a Negro had to be a night thing and its aura of uneasiness had to be countered by gallows humor.

What did we fear? I could not say exactly. It was unlikely the Klan would come riding down on us. We merely fell into the fear that hangs over the state, a nameless and awful thing. It reminded me of the nagging, focusless terror we felt in Europe when Hitler began his marches, the terror of talking with Jews (and our deep shame of it). For the Negro, at least, this fear is ever-present in the South, and the same is doubtlessly true of many decent whites who watch and wait, and feel the deep shame of it.

Once inside their home, the awkwardness gradually lessened. However, it was painful for me. I could not accustom myself to sitting in their living room as an "equal."

They have a modest home, but it was a palace compared to the places I had lived in recently. Most striking, however, was the atmosphere of easiness, of trust and warmth. It came as a new revelation to me: the simple ability to enjoy the pleasures of one's home, to relax and feel at ease. Though ordinary to most men, this was a luxury virtually unknown in my experience as a Negro.

The Easts showed me to my room and suggested I might like to wash up. I noted as another example of gallows humor that Billie had put out black guest towels and washcloth for me.

We discussed our experiences until late in the night. We talked of our mutual friend, the literary historian Maxwell Geismar, who had introduced us by correspondence a year ago. P. D. had recently visited in the Geismar home; he told me of the great help Max and Anne Geismar had solicited over the country for him.

Then East fetched the manuscript of his autobiography, *The Magnolia Jungle,* which Simon & Schuster is publishing. At midnight I took the manuscript to my room, intending to glance through it before sleeping.

I could not put the manuscript down. I read through the night the story of a native-born Southerner, a man who had tried to follow the crowd, who ran an innocuous little newspaper, *The Petal Paper,* glad-handed, joined the local civic clubs and kept himself in line with "popular opinion," which meant "popular prejudice," or "keep the nigger in his place," in a Christian and 100 per cent American fair-play manner, of course.

"I glad-handed from hell to breakfast, winning friends and conning people," he wrote. He adopted the Southern editorial policy, "Love American motherhood and hate sin" and never mention Negroes except in a manner harmonious to the Southern Way of Life. *The Petal Paper* carried local news along with short features such as "Citizen of the Week" and "Prayer and Meditation." This latter, written by local ministers, was "aimed at those Christians who were afraid not to read any printed word about Jesus."

For the first year, East had managed to please everyone and offend no one. The paper had prospered. He had made money and he was popular among the townspeople.

East had fence-straddled all major issues, if he mentioned them at all. At night he began to have trouble sleeping, to feel he was prostituting his conscience and his editorial responsibilities. "When I'd become aware of my state of mind, I would be frightened and snap back with a healthy smile and a hearty handshake. Such is the effect of the sweet smell of money."

More and more tormented, East entered a battle with his conscience, his sense of decency. It became clear to him that though he wrote in his paper what his readers wanted to see, this was not always the truth. As the situation in the South degenerated after the 1954 Supreme Court decision on segregation, he was faced with a choice—either he must continue more and more to alter truth to make it conform to people's comfort, or he must write the truth in the dim hope that people would alter their comfort to conform to it.

His editorials began to lean away from the "correct" Southern attitude. He used the word "fair" to describe his new editorial policy. "I thought honestly and sincerely that with rare exception a man could say what he wished without fear of reprisal, especially a man with a newspaper who was seeking to expand his commercial and unhappy soul in a direction that was, for a rare change, decent and honest." His decision to be *fair* was not in keeping with the "correct" Southern attitude.

He continued stubbornly to preach justice. He said that in order to prove that the Negroes have no right to their freedoms, we are subverting the very principles that preserve the spirit of our own . . . we are endangering ourselves, no matter what our race and creed.

In essence, he asked for ethical and virtuous social conduct. He said that before we can have justice, we must first have truth, and he insisted on his right and duty to print the truth. Significantly, this was considered high treason.

I lay in the bed, under a lamp, and read and smoked cigarettes. Through the wall of the room, I heard P. D. East snore, but in here he was much awake on the pages.

He was threatened and hounded by anonymous callers. The Citizens Councils found him worthy of their attention, after which he lost most of his local subscribers and ads.

In a country of free speech and press, they starved him out for expressing views not in harmony with their prejudices.

For example, he questioned a bill proposed in the state legislature that would authorize use of tax funds to support the White Citizens Councils. He asked if it is fair to take tax money from the Negro and then use it to support an organization set up for the avowed purpose of supressing him.

Another bill, to levy penalizing fines against any church holding nonsegregated services, was, he contended, in flagrant contradiction to the First Amendment of the Constitution.

He pointed out that these were simply the old story of legalized injustice. The local state legislature (in opposition to constitutional law), insisted that whatever it decided was *de jure* law, a position that wipes out the distinction between true and false judgments. "For," as Burke said, "if the judgment makes the law and not the law directs the judgment, it is impossible there should be such a thing as an illegal judgment given." A law is not good merely because the legislature wills it, but the legislature has the mortal duty to will only that which is good.

This tendency to make laws that are convenient or advantageous rather than right has mushroomed in Southern legislatures. It has produced laws of a cynicism scarcely believable in a civilized society. Even when these have been tested and thrown out as illegal by superior courts, they have in some instances continued to be enforced because "they haven't taken them off the dockets."

Subscriptions were canceled. Ads were canceled. As a result of my host's campaign for nothing more than fairness or "couthness," as he came to call it, even his old friends, swayed by the pressures put on them by society, turned against him. He began getting telephone calls telling him he was a "goddamn nigger-loving, Jew-loving, communist son-of-a-bitch." Wherever he went he carried a gun.

"My reaction was as it had been before and as it was to be many times in days to come. I was depressed to the point that I went into my room at home, sat on the side of the bed and wept like a baby."

It was an odd manuscript; in the midst of the profoundest personal tragedy, sinking into economic ruin, he wrote brilliantly funny columns. His finest attacks have been to take the "true Southerner's" viewpoint and render it absurd, all in seeming to defend and explain it. Tragedy turned him into one of the subtlest and sharpest satirists in American letters. In *The Magnolia Jungle* the juxtaposition of the best of these columns against a background of stark horror gives a striking effect. It shows the phenomenon of a man living at his lowest and writing at his highest; a grief-stricken man who turns out monstrously funny copy. Like Monoculus, he poked fun at the devil.

His case, along with those of other "Southern traitors," like Hodding Carter, Easton King, Ralph McGill and Mark Ethridge, illustrates the "true Southerner's" admirable lack of race prejudice: he is as willing to destroy whites who question his "wisdom" as he is to destroy Negroes.

I put the manuscript away and tried to sleep. But the sun poured into my window. I had read all night.

▼   ▼   ▼

NOVEMBER 15

I had hardly dozed when East came into the room with a lone cup of coffee on a serving tray. Groggily, I asked him the time. It was seven thirty. My body pleaded for sleep, but I knew he wanted to discuss the manuscript.

It was an odd, exhausting day. We spent it in the office he has at his home. I drank cups of coffee and listened to Mozart quintets and read the portions of the script he had cut out. In many instances I urged him to restore these deletions—but it was insane. I was sleepy, I was preoccupied with the magnificent music and I was trying to read while P. D. talked—a long, immensely funny monologue, punctuated every five minutes by: "Well, I'll shut up now and let you concentrate on that. But did Max ever tell you about . . ." And it would be another story.

"I was supposed to go to Dillard and give a lecture Monday," he said sadly.

"Are you going?"

"No . . . Dean Gandy asked me to come. I begged him to let me postpone it a while. Told him I was busy working on the book. And that understanding sonofabitch *agreed;* didn't even insist. Said 'Certainly, P. D., the book comes first. We can have you a bit later.' It hurt my feelings."

"Hell, he was just being nice."

"Nice—hell." He grimaced with pain. "He didn't act a bit broken up because I put him off. Well—you just stay over till Monday and I'll drive you back to New Orleans. I'll drop by and see him and show him I could have been had if he'd just had the basic common decency to insist."

We worked all day, going through his files. He piled research material, hate pamphlets, news clippings, letters and other items on my bed for me to study at night. We broke off at intervals to visit with his wife, Billie, and their young daughter, Karen, who, learning that I was from Texas and lived on a farm, called me "that rich bald-headed Texas rancher." Except for two Jewish families, they are ostracized from society in Hattiesburg. Billie spends much of her time fishing in a nearby tank in the afternoons—a lonely existence. Karen is an extraordinarily beautiful blond child, the same age as my daughter and much like her. She is bright, outrageously outspoken and tender. She and her father were constantly at war over the TV programs. I could make little sense of it, except that the arguments were long and full of recriminations on both sides; but the traditional roles were reversed. She did not approve of her father's avid watching of westerns and children's programs, and he insisted that he be allowed, by God, to view his "favorites."

I left them around eleven and meant to fall into bed. But the material P. D. had placed on the two bed tables fascinated me so that I studied it and made notes without sleeping until dawn. It is perhaps the most incredible collection of what East calls "assdom" in the South. It shows that the most obscene figures are not the ignorant ranting racists, but the legal minds who front for them, who "invent" for them the legislative proposals and the propaganda bulletins. They deliberately choose to foster distortions, always under the guise of patriotism, upon a people who have no means of checking the facts. Their appeals are to regional interest, showing complete contempt for privacy of conscience, and a willingness to destroy and subvert values that have traditionally been held supreme in this land.

▼ ▼ ▼

NOVEMBER 16

Though the trip from New Orleans to Hattiesburg had seemed interminable on the bus, the return to New Orleans in P. D.'s car was quickly done. P. D. took me to Dillard University, one of the two Negro universities in New Orleans. A green, spacious campus with white buildings, great trees streaming Spanish moss. We drove through slowly, of necessity, since the campus drives have cement ridges every forty or fifty feet that would cause your car to bump badly if any speed were attempted. P. D. cursed these richly and made the typical "Southern white" remarks about "Did you ever see such a damn beautiful campus for a bunch of *niggers*. They're getting uppityer and uppityer."

He stopped deep in the campus at the cottages provided for the faculty and we went in to meet Dean Sam Gandy. The Dean, a handsome, cultivated man of great wit, had just returned from a trip. Almost before we were introduced, P. D. launched into bitter complaints, wanting to know why Dean Gandy had not insisted he give the lecture today.

"But you told me you were simply too busy," Gandy laughed. "Naturally we wanted you, but . . ."

Placated, P. D. and I confided my project to the Dean and his beautiful wife. Though we had little time to discuss it, since the Dean had to be at his office for an appointment, I promised to return and share my findings with him. We went to the car, which P. D. carefully and ostentatiously pretended to unlock.

"Why, P. D., what on earth did you lock your car for here in this cloistered atmosphere?" Gandy asked.

P. D. looked shifty-eyed, distrustful, in both directions, and then in a loud stage whisper said: "Well, with all these damn nigras hanging around, you know . . ."

Gandy bent double with laughter and outrage. He asked P. D. how the voting situation was in Mississippi and P. D. told the story of the Negro who went to register. The white man taking his application gave him the standard literacy tests:

"What is the first line of the thirty-second paragraph of the United States Constitution?" he asked.

The applicant answered perfectly.

"Name the eleventh President of the United States and his entire cabinet."

The applicant answered correctly.

Finally, unable to trip him up, the white man asked, "Can you read and write?"

The applicant wrote his name and was then handed a newspaper in Chinese to test his reading. He studied it carefully for a time.

"Well, can you read it?"

"I can read the headline, but I can't make out the body text."

Incredulous, the white man said: "You can read *that* headline?"

"Oh, yes, I've got the meaning all right."

"What's it say?"

"It says this is one Negro in Mississippi who's not going to get to vote this year."

East let me out of the car in downtown New Orleans, on Canal Street. I bought a meal of beans and rice in the nearby Negro Café and then went to the bus station to purchase a ticket back into Mississippi, but this time to the coastal town of Biloxi. I did not see the lady who gave

me the hate stare a few days earlier. With three hours to
kill until bus time, I walked and window-shopped on Canal.
The town was decorated for Christmas and I felt lost in
the great crowds. A cool, sunlit afternoon. I looked at all
the children coming and going in the stores, most of them
excited to see Santa Claus, and I felt the greatest longing
to see my own.

Once again I stopped men on the street and asked directions to the French Market or to some church, and once
again each gave me courteous replies. Despite the in-
equalities, I liked New Orleans, perhaps because I dreaded
so the prospect of leaving once more to go into the Deep
South, perhaps because it was, after all, so much better
here than in Mississippi—though I understand that the rest
of Louisiana is scarcely any better.

At the Jesuit church, I picked up a booklet I had also
noticed on Dean Gandy's coffee table—*For Men of Good
Will*, by Father Robert Guste. Penciled across the top in
red were the words "Racial Justice." I stood in the sunlight outside the church, noticing that passers-by either
lifted their hats or made a discreet sign of the cross on their
chests as they came abreast of the church. I flipped through
the pages, noticing the dedication:

Dedicated to My Dad and Mother and to the countless other
Southern parents and educators who sincerely try to instill in
their children and their students a love for all men and a respect for the dignity and worth of every man.

Father Guste, a parish priest of the Archdiocese of New
Orleans, born and reared in the South, wrote the book to
clarify the problems of racial justice for those "men of good
will" who are sincerely alarmed by "the Problem."

I glanced through quickly and promised myself a
thorough reading. Suddenly it occurred to me that I made
a strange and too obvious picture there—a large Negro,
standing in front of a church, absorbed in a pamphlet on
racial justice. I quickly dropped it into my jacket and
walked to the Greyhound station to wait for my bus.

In the rest room, I saw the remains of a loaf of French
bread lying on the floor beside the waste bin. It told the

story of some poor devil who had come there, closed himself in the cubicle and eaten his meal of half a loaf. The small room was perfectly clean except for a placard attached to the back of the door. I read the neatly typed NOTICE! until I saw that it was only another list of prices a white man would pay for various types of sensuality with various ages of Negro girls. The whites frequently walk into colored rest rooms, Scotch-tape these notices to the wall. This man offered his services free to any Negro woman over twenty, offered to pay, on an ascending scale, from two dollars for a nineteen-year-old girl up to seven fifty for a fourteen-year-old and more for perversion dates. He gave a contact point for later in the evening and urged any Negro man who wanted to earn five dollars for himself to find him a date within this price category. He would probably have success, I thought, glancing at the butt of bread. To a man who had nothing to eat but bread and perhaps a piece of cheese in a public rest room, five dollars could mean a great deal. I wondered about the Negro who had left this trace of his passing. What sort of man was he? A derelict? No, a derelict would have left an empty wine bottle. Someone who could not find work and had grown too hungry to wait for something better? Probably. If the woman in the Catholic Book Store had not cashed my travelers check, I might have been reduced to the same thing. What astonished me was that he had not carried the remains of the bread with him. Perhaps he, too, had seen the notice on the door and counted on five dollars for a decent supper.

A young man entered as I dried my hands. He nodded politely, with a quick, intelligent expression, glanced at the notice and snorted with amusement and derision. In these matters, the Negro has seen the backside of the white man too long to be shocked. He feels an indulgent superiority whenever he sees these evidences of the white man's frailty. This is one of the sources of his chafing at being considered inferior. He cannot understand how the white man can show the most demeaning aspects of his nature and at the same time delude himself into thinking he is inherently superior. To the Negro who sees this element of the white man's nature—and he sees it much more often than any other—the white man's comments about the Negro's alleged "immorality" ring maddeningly hollow.

▼ ▼ ▼

NOVEMBER 19

I arrived by bus in Biloxi too late to find any Negroes about, so I walked inland and slept, half-freezing, in a tin-roofed shed with an open south front. In the morning I found breakfast in a little Negro café—coffee and toast—and then walked down to the highway to begin hitching. The highway ran for miles along some of the most magnificent beaches I have ever seen—white sands, a beautiful ocean; and opposite the beach, splendid homes. The sun warmed me through, and I took my time, stopping to study the historic markers placed along the route.

For lunch, I bought a pint of milk and a ready-wrapped bologna sandwich in a roadside store. I carried them to the walk that runs along the shallow sea wall and ate. A local Negro stopped to talk. I asked him if the swimming were good there, since the beaches were so splendid. He told me the beaches were "man-made," the sand dredged in; but that unless a Negro sneaked off to some isolated spot, he'd never know how the water was, since Negroes weren't permitted to enjoy the beaches. He pointed out the injustice of this policy, since the upkeep of the beaches comes from a gasoline tax. "In other words, every time we buy a gallon of gas, we pay a penny to keep the beach up so the whites can use it," he said. He added that some of the local Negro citizens were considering a project to keep an account of the gasoline they purchased throughout the year and at the end of that time demand from the town fathers either a refund on their gasoline tax or the privilege of using the beaches for which they had paid their fair part.

After a time I walked again on legs that grew weak with weariness. A car pulled up beside me and a young, red-headed white man told me to "hop in." His glance was friendly, courteous, and he spoke with no condescension. I began to hope that I had underestimated the people of Mississippi. With what eagerness I grasped at every straw of kindness, wanting to give a good report.

"Beautiful country, isn't it?" he said.

"Marvelous."

"You just passing through?"

"Yes sir . . . I'm on my way to Mobile."

"Where you from?"

"Texas."

"I'm from Massachusetts," he said, as though he were eager for me to know he was not a Mississippian. I felt the keenest disappointment, and mentally erased the passages I had mentally composed about the kindness of the Mississippian who gave the Negro a ride. He told me he had no sympathy for the "Southern attitude."

"That shows," I said.

"But you know," he added, "these are some of the finest people in the world about everything else."

"I'm sure they are."

"I know you won't believe it—but it's really the truth. I just don't ever talk to them about the race question."

"With your attitude, I can understand that," I laughed.

"They can't discuss it," he said. "It's a shame but all they do is get mad whenever you bring it up. I'll never understand it. They're blocked on that one subject. I've lived here over five years now—and they're good neighbors; but if I mention race with any sympathy for the Negro, they just tell me I'm an 'outsider' and don't understand about Negroes. What's there to understand?"

I walked what—ten, fifteen miles? I walked because one does not just simply sit down in the middle of a highway, because there was nothing to do but walk.

Late in the afternoon, my mind hazed with fatigue. I concentrated all my energy in putting one foot in front of the other. Sweat poured down into my eyes and soaked my clothes and the heat of the pavement came through my shoes. I remember I stopped at a little custard stand and bought a dish of ice cream merely to have the excuse to sit at one of the tables under the trees—none of which were occupied. But before I could take my ice cream and walk to one of them some white teen-agers appeared and took seats. I dared not sit down even at a distant table. Wretched with disappointment I leaned against a tree and ate the ice cream.

Behind the custard stand stood an old unpainted privy leaning badly to one side. I returned to the dispensing window of the stand.

"Yes sir," the white man said congenially. "You want something else?"

"Where's the nearest rest room I could use?" I asked.

He brushed his white, brimless cook's cap back and rubbed his forefinger against his sweaty forehead. "Let's see. You can go on up there to the bridge and then cut down the road to the left . . . and just follow that road. You'll come to a little settlement—there's some stores and gas stations there."

"How far is it?" I asked, pretending to be in greater discomfort than I actually was.

"Not far—thirteen, maybe fourteen blocks."

A locust's lazy rasping sawed the air from the nearby oak trees.

"Isn't there anyplace closer?" I said, determined to see if he would not offer me the use of the dilapidated outhouse, which certainly no human could degrade any more than time and the elements had.

His seamed face showed the concern and sympathy of one human for another in a predicament every man understands. "I can't think of any . . ." he said slowly.

I glanced around the side toward the outhouse. "Any chance of me running in there for a minute?"

"Nope," he said—clipped, final, soft, as though he regretted it but could never permit such a thing. "I'm sorry." He turned away.

"Thank you just the same," I said.

By dark I was away from the beach area and out in the country. Strangely, I began getting rides. Men would pass you in daylight but pick you up after dark.

I must have had a dozen rides that evening. They blear into a nightmare, the one scarcely distinguishable from the other.

It quickly became obvious why they picked me up. All but two picked me up the way they would pick up a pornographic photograph or book—except that this was verbal pornography. With a Negro, they assumed they need give no semblance of self-respect or respectability. The visual element entered into it. In a car at night visibility is reduced. A man will reveal himself in the dark, which gives an illusion of anonymity, more than he will in the bright light. Some were shamelessly open, some shamelessly subtle. All showed morbid curiosity about the sexual life of the Negro, and all had, at base, the same stereotyped image of the Negro as an inexhaustible sex-machine with oversized genitals and a vast store of experiences, immensely varied. They appeared to think that the Negro has done all of those "special" things they themselves have never dared to do. They carried the conversation into the depths of depravity. I note these things because it is harrowing to see decent-looking men and boys assume that because a man is black they need show him none of the reticences they would, out of respect, show the most derelict white man. I note them, too, because they differed completely from the "bull sessions" men customarily have among themselves. These latter, no matter how frank, have generally a robust tone that says: "We are men, this is an enjoyable thing to do and to discuss, but it will never impugn the basic respect we give one another; it will never distort our humanity." In this, the atmosphere, no matter how coarse, has a verve and an essential joviality that casts out morbidity. It implies respect for the persons involved. But all that I could see here were men shorn of respect either for themselves or their companion.

In my grogginess and exhaustion, these conversations became ghoulish. Each time one of them let me out of his car, I hoped the next would spare me his pantings. I remained mute and pleaded my exhaustion and lack of sleep.

"I'm so tired, I just can't think," I would say.

Like men who had promised themselves pleasure, they would not be denied. It became a strange sort of hounding as they nudged my skull for my sexual reminiscences.

"Well, did you ever do such-and-such?"

"I don't know . . ." I moaned.

"What's the matter—haven't you got any manhood? My old man told me you wasn't really a man till you'd done such-and-such."

Or the older ones, hardened, cynical in their lechery. "Now, don't try to kid me. I wasn't born yesterday. You know you've done such-and-such, just like I have. Hell, it's good that way. Tell me, did you ever get a white woman?"

"Do you think I'm crazy?" I tacitly denied the racist's contention, for he would not hesitate to use it against the Negroes in his conversations around town: "Why, I had one of them admit to me just last night that he craves white women."

"I didn't ask if you was crazy," he said. "I asked if you ever had one—or ever really wanted one." Then, conniving, sweet-toned, "There's plenty white women would like to have a good buck Negro."

"A Negro'd be asking for the rope to get himself mixed up with white women."

"You're just telling me that, but I'll bet inside you think differently . . ."

"This is sure beautiful country through here. What's the main crop?"

"*Don't* you? You can tell me. Hell, I don't care."

"No sir," I sighed.

"You're lying in your teeth and you know it."

Silence. Soon after, almost abruptly he halted the car and said, "Okay, this is as far as I go." He spoke as though he resented my uncooperative attitude, my refusal to give him this strange verbal sexual pleasure.

I thanked him for the ride and stepped down onto the highway. He drove on in the same direction.

Soon another picked me up, a young man in his late twenties who spoke with an educated flair. His questions had the spurious elevation of a scholar seeking information, but the information he sought was entirely sexual, and presupposed that in the ghetto the Negro's life is one of marathon sex with many different partners, open to the view of all; in a word, that marital fidelity and sex as love's goal of union with the beloved object were exclusively the white man's property. Though he pretended to be above such ideas as racial superiority and spoke with genuine warmth, the entire context of his talk reeked of preconceived ideas to the contrary.

"I understand Negroes are much more broad-minded about such things," he said warmly.

"I don't know."

"I understand you make more of an art—or maybe *hobby* out of your sex than we do."

"I doubt it."

"Well, you people don't seem to have the inhibitions we have. We're all basically puritans. I understand Negroes do a lot more things—different kinds of sex—than we do. Oh, don't get me wrong. I admire your attitude, think it's basically healthier than ours. You don't get so damned many *conflicts*. Negroes don't have much neuroses, do they? I mean you people have a more realistic tradition about sex—you're not so sheltered from it as we are."

I knew that what he really meant was that Negroes grew up seeing it from infancy. He had read the same stories, the same reports of social workers about parents sharing a room with children, the father coming home drunk and forcing the mother onto the bed in full view of the young ones. I felt like laughing in his face when I thought of the Negro families I had known already as a Negro: the men on the streets, in the ghettos, the housewives and their great concern that their children "grow up right."

"You people regard sex as a *total* experience—and that's how it should be. Anything that makes you feel good is morally all right for you. Isn't that the main difference?"

"I don't think there's any difference," I said cautiously, not wanting to test the possibility of his wrath at having a Negro disagree with him.

"You *don't?*" His voice betrayed excitement and eagerness; gave no hint of offense.

"Our ministers preach sin and hell just as much as yours," I said. "We've got the same puritanical background as you. We worry just as much as white people about our children losing their virginity or being perverted. We've got the same miserable little worries and problems over our sexual effectiveness, the same guilts that you have."

He appeared astonished and delighted, not at what I said but at the fact that I could say it. His whole attitude of enthusiasm practically shouted, "Why, you talk *intelligently!*" He was so obtuse he did not realize the implied insult in his astonishment that a black man could do anything but say "yes sir" and mumble four-letter words.

Again, he asked questions scarcely different from those that white men would ask themselves; especially scholars who would discuss cultural differences on a detached plane. Yet here the tone was subtly conniving. He went through the motions of courteous research, but he could not hide his real preoccupation. He asked about the size of Negro genitalia and the details of Negro sex life. Only the language differed from the previous inquirers—the substance was the same. The difference was that here I could disagree with him without risking a flood of abuse or petulance. He quoted Kinsey and others. It became apparent he was one of those young men who possess an impressive store of facts, but no truths. This again would have no significance and would be unworthy of note except for one thing: I have talked with such men many times as a white and they never show the glow of prurience he revealed. The significance lay in the fact that my blackness and his concepts of what my blackness implied allowed him to expose himself in this manner. He saw the Negro as a different species. He saw me as something akin to an animal in that he felt no need to maintain his sense of human dignity, though certainly he would have denied this.

I told myself that I was tired, that I must not judge these men who picked me up and for the price of a ride submitted me to the swamps of their fantasy lives. They showed me something that all men have but seldom bring to the surface, since most men seek health. The boy ended up wanting me to expose myself to him, saying he had never seen a Negro naked. I turned mute, indrawn, giving no answer. The silence rattled between us and I felt sorry for the reprimand that grew from me to him in the silence. I did not want this cruelty to him, since I knew that he showed me a side of his nature that was special to the night and the situation, a side rarely brought to light in his everyday living. I stared at the dimly lighted car dashboard and saw him attending an aunt's funeral, having Sunday dinner with his parents, doing some kindness for a friend—for he was kind. How could I let him see that I understood and that I still respected him, and that I formed no judgment against him for this momentary slip? For instead of seeing it as a manifestation of some poor human charity, he might view it as confirmation that Negroes are insensitive to sexual aberration, that they think nothing of it—and this would carry on the legend that has so handicapped the Negro.

"I wasn't going to do anything to you," he said in a voice lifeless with humiliation. "I'm not a queer or anything."

"Of course not," I said. "It's nothing."

"It's just that I don't get a chance to talk to educated Negroes—people that can answer questions."

"You make it more complicated than it is," I said. "If you want to know about the sexual morals of the Negro —his practices and ideals—it's no mystery. These are human matters, and the Negro is the same human as the white man. Just ask yourself how it is for a white man and you'll know all the answers. Negro trash is the same as white trash. Negro decency is about the same, too."

"But there are differences. The social studies I've read . . ."

"They don't deal with any basic difference in human nature between black and white," I said. "They only study the effects of environment on human nature. You place the white man in the ghetto, deprive him of educational advantages, arrange it so he has to struggle hard to fulfill his instinct for self-respect, give him little physical privacy and less leisure, and he would after a time assume the same characteristics you attach to the Negro. These characteristics don't spring from whiteness or blackness, but from a man's conditioning."

"Yes, but Negroes have more illegitimate children, earlier loss of virginity and more crime—these are established facts," he insisted without unkindness.

"The fact that the white race has the same problems proves these are not Negro characteristics, but the product of our condition as men," I said. "When you force humans into a subhuman mode of existence, this always happens. Deprive a man of any contact with the pleasures of the spirit and he'll fall completely into those of the flesh."

"But we don't deprive you people of the 'pleasures of the spirit,' " he said.

"In most places we can't go to the concerts, the theater, the museums, public lectures . . . or even to the library. Our schools in the South don't compare to the white schools, poor as they are. You deprive a man of educational opportunities and he'll have no knowledge of the great civilizing influences of art, history, literature and philosophy. Many Negroes don't even know these things exist. With practically nothing to exalt the mind or exercise the spirit, any man is going to sink to his lowest depths. It becomes vicious—and tragic."

"I can't imagine how it must be," he said. "I don't think it's fair. But just the same, plenty of whites don't have access to these things—to art, history, literature and philosophy. Some of the finest people I know live in the country where they never get to museums, concerts."

"Living in the country, they are surrounded by natural museums and concerts," I said. "Besides, those doors are always open to them. The Negro, too, fares better in the country. But most are deprived of education. Ignorance keeps them poor, and when a town-dwelling Negro is poor, he lives in the ghetto. His wife has to work usually, and this leaves the children without parental companionship. In such places, where all of man's time is spent just surviving, he rarely knows what it means to read a great book. He has grown up and now sees his children grow up in squalor. His wife usually earns more than he. He is thwarted in his need to be father-of-the-household. When he looks at his children and his home, he feels the guilt of not having given them something better. His only salvation is not to give a damn finally, or else he will fall into despair. In despair a man's sense of virtue is dulled. He no longer cares. He will do anything to escape it—steal or commit acts of violence—or perhaps try to lose himself in sensuality. Most often the sex-king is just a poor devil trying to prove the manhood that his whole existence denies. This is what the whites call the 'sorry nigger.' Soon he will either desert his home or become so unbearable he is kicked out. This leaves the mother to support the children alone. To keep food in their bellies, she has to spend most of her time away from them, working. This leaves the children to the streets, prey to any sight, any conversation, any sexual experiment that comes along to make their lives more interesting or pleasurable. To a young girl who has nothing, has never known anything, the baubles she can get—both in a kind of crude affection and in gifts or money—by granting sex to a man or boy appeal to her as toys to a child. She gets pregnant sometimes and then the vicious circle is given impetus. In some instances the mother cannot make enough to support her children, so she sells her sex for what she can get. This gets easier and easier until she comes up with still another child to abort or support. But none of this is 'Negro-ness.' "

"I don't know . . ." he sighed. "It looks like a man could do better."

"It looks that way to you, because you can see what would be better. The Negro knows something is terribly wrong, but with things the way they are, he can't know that something better actually exists on the other side of work and study. We are all born blank. It's the same for blacks or whites or any other shade of man. Your blanks have been filled in far differently from those of a child grown up in the filth and poverty of the ghetto."

He drove without speaking through a thundershower that crinkled the windshield and raised the hum of his tires an octave.

"But the situation is changing," I said after a time. "The Negro may not understand exactly *how,* but he knows one thing—the only way out of this tragedy is through education, training. Thousands of them sacrifice everything to get the education, to prove once and for all that the Negro's capacity for learning, for accomplishment, is equal to that of any other man—that the pigment has nothing to do with degrees of intelligence, talent or virtue. This isn't just wishful thinking. It's been proved conclusively in every field."

"We don't hear about those things," he said.

"I know. Southern newspapers print every rape, attempted rape, suspected rape and 'maybe rape,' but outstanding accomplishment is not considered newsworthy. Even the Southern Negro has little chance to know this, since he reads the same slanted reports in the newspapers."

The young man slowed to a halt in a little settlement to let me out.

"I'm sorry about a while ago—I don't know what got into me," he said.

"I've already forgotten it."

"No offense?"

"No offense."

"Okay. Good luck to you."

I thanked him and stepped out onto the wet neon reflections of the road. The air, cool and mist-filled, surrounded me with its freshness. I watched the red taillight of his car fog into the distance.

I had no time to worry about sitting down or getting a sandwich. An old-model car tooted its horn and skidded to a stop a few yards beyond me. The smell of a rainy Alabama night, the succession of sexual oddments turned me suddenly sick with dread at what this stranger would want. But I had no alternative. There was no place there to sleep.

"Where you going?" he asked.

"Mobile," I said. He told me to get in. I glanced through the glassless window to see a heavy-set, round-faced, tough-looking young man.

As we drove, the tensions drained from me. He was boisterous, loud and guileless. I could only conclude that he was color blind, since he appeared totally unaware that I was a Negro. He enjoyed company, nothing more. He told me he was a construction worker and tonight he was late getting home to his wife and infant son. "I couldn't get this sonofabitching rattletrap to go," he said. "I leave the good car at home for my wife."

For an hour we delighted ourselves with talk of our

children. The experience of parenthood filled him with enthusiasm and he recited the endless merits of his son and drew me out to tell him of my children.

"I can see I'm not going to make it without something to eat," he said. "I'm usually home by six and my wife has supper on the table. You had any supper?"

"No, I sure haven't."

"You want a hamburger?"

"I don't think there's anyplace here that would serve me."

"Shit, I'll bring it to the car. We can eat while I'm driving."

I watched him walk into a roadside café. He looked young, not over twenty, and I wondered how he had escaped the habit of guarded fencing that goes on constantly between whites and Negroes in the South wherever they meet. He was the first man I met of either color who did not confuse the popular image of the thing with the thing itself.

I wondered where he got this, and sought to discover the source of his attitude during the drive into Mobile. His background, his education and his home were ordinary. On the car radio he played with relish the twang-twang blues type of music and his TV preferences were westerns. "Oh, hell, I can't go for those old heavy dramas." Perhaps his religion? "My wife's a Presbyterian. Sometimes I go with her. But I don't much like it." Perhaps his reading?

"Have you got a good library in Mobile?"

"I don't know, to tell you the truth. I think it's supposed to be pretty good. My wife reads a lot."

I could only conclude that his attitude came from an overwhelming love for his child, so profound it spilled over to all humanity. I knew that he was totally unaware of its ability to cure men; of the blessing it could be to someone like me after having been exhausted and scraped raw in my heart by others this rainy Alabama night.

I thought of Maritain's conclusion that the only solution to the problems of man is the return of charity (in the old embracing sense of *caritas,* not in the stingy literal sense it has assumed in our language and in our days) and metaphysics. Or, more simply, the maxim of St. Augustine: "Love, and then do what you will."

To live in a world where men do not love, where they cheat and are callous, is to sink into a preoccupation with death, and to see the futility of anything except virtue. When I crossed the line from Mississippi into Alabama, I felt as though I were leaving a cemetery.

Since I knew little of the Mobile of today, my young friend let me out downtown near the bus center. Across the street from the bus station, I saw an elderly Negro man seated on a door stoop near the curb. I went over and sat beside him. We talked casually for a time. He said he preached at a little street mission nearby. I asked him where I could find a room for the night. He put his head close to mine and studied me through thick glasses under the street lamp. After asking if I were a "nice man," he offered to let me bunk with him. He told me he occupied the two front rooms of the house where his daughter's family lived.

We bought hamburgers for supper and took the bus to his home, eating on the way.

"It's not much, but you're welcome to stay here," he said when he opened the door and turned on the lights. His two rooms were furnished only with an upright piano, a straight chair, a small table and an unmade double bed. His courtesy was simple and easy. He picked up dirty clothes and old newspapers without apology. Then, while I unpacked my duffel, he went outside and returned with a large metal washtub. Refusing my help, he filled it with buckets of water from the back of the house. He offered to let me bathe, but seeing how much trouble it was to haul the water, I declined.

While he bathed, I sat on the bed in the other room and made notes. The walls had been covered with cheesecloth but never papered. Gray planking showed through the gauze. Above the bed he had pinned a calendar-reproduction of "Christ in the Temple." Thumbtacked to the doorframe were photos of his family. His extra clothing hung from nails driven into the wall. A fluffy new beige-colored bath mat at the side of the bed was the only floor covering. Despite its poverty, the room had a bare brightness.

My host, unlike most Negroes, did not use the more economical low-watt bulbs. He lighted his rooms brilliantly. I heard his footsteps and the drip of water on the floor as he stepped out.

I remained seated until I heard him begin to drag the tub across the floor. When I stepped in to help him, he was dressed only in a pair of wrinkled khaki pants. We carried the tub out and emptied it under a chinaberry tree in the side yard.

We undressed and prepared to go to bed in our underwear. He removed the small black Bible from his coat pocket and kissed it unself-consciously before placing it at the rear of the table. The only other book I noted—or reading material of any sort—was a paperback mystery standing upright between two Oriental book ends on top of the piano.

He waited for me to crawl into the bed before switching off the light. I heard his bare feet on the floor and felt his weight as he settled into bed beside me. In a moment he was up again. Though the night was cold, he opened the front door so we could have some fresh air. From a distant radio I heard the desolating music of a dance orchestra.

"Do you want to talk or sleep?" he asked when he returned to the bed. His voice sounded startlingly close in the dark, after my ear had become accustomed to the radio music outside.

"Let's talk a while," I said, feeling the depression of the night and the poverty close in on the room.

But talk banished the somberness. He spoke of the Lord with relish. We lay there in the darkness under quilts, our voices bouncing back from the bare walls; and we chuckled and had a great time talking about the miracles. We marveled at the raising up of Lazarus.

"That ain't every day, eh, Mr. Griffin?" he said, and nudged my arm with his elbow. "Don't you wish you could've seen the look on their faces when they saw that dead man get up?" He burst out laughing. "After he's been dead *four whole days*. God almighty!"

Later we talked about the South. He had sent two sons away to study law. They would never return. "If I could

have foreseen ten years ago how things would happen, I'd
have cleared out too. I'm too old now. And besides, I've
got my daughters and grandchildren here."

"But surely your sons will come back to see you."

"I don't want them to. They'll come back for my funeral.
That's the worst part of this devilment. If the young ones
want a decent life, they've got to go somewhere else. All
the families are being split up. That's the shame of it."

We spoke of the whites. "They're God's children, just
like us," he said. "Even if they don't act very godlike any
more. God tells us straight—we've got to love them, no *ifs,
ands,* and *buts* about it. Why, if we hated them, we'd be
sunk down to their level. There's plenty of us doing just
that, too."

"A lot of the people I've talked to think we've turned
the other cheek too long," I said.

"You can't get around what's right, though," he said.
"When we stop loving them, that's when they win."

"How's that?"

"Then they'll have ruined our race for sure. They'll
have dragged us down plumb to the bottom."

"Are you just supposed to let them carry on then?"

"No . . . we can't do that any longer. We're supposed
to get our rights in a proper way. And try to understand
that it's hard for them, too, to change around from the
old ways. We've got plenty of old Uncle Toms that don't
want things changed any more than the whites. You can
give them two dollars and they'll pull the string that sends
us all to hell. They're a disgrace to our race. And then
we've got plenty of young smart-aleck people that don't
want nothing except the chance to 'get even' with the whites
. . . they're full of hate and piss and it's a God's shame.
They're just as much Judases as the Uncle Toms."

As always, the conversation stalemated with "None of
it really makes any sense."

▼ ▼ ▼

Three days in Mobile. I spent them walking through the town, searching jobs, and then every night I met my host on the corner opposite the bus station and we went to his house to sleep.

Again, an important part of my daily life was spent searching for the basic things that all whites take for granted: a place to eat, or somewhere to find a drink of water, a rest room, somewhere to wash my hands. More than once I walked into drugstores where a Negro can buy cigarettes or anything else except soda fountain service. I asked politely where I might find a glass of water. Though they had water not three yards away, they carefully directed me to the nearest Negro café. Had I asked outright for a drink, they would perhaps have given it. But I never asked. The Negro dreads rejection, and I waited for them to offer the drink. Not one ever did. No matter where you are, the nearest Negro café is always far away, it seems. I learned to eat a great deal when it was available and convenient, because it might not be available or convenient when the belly next indicated its hunger. I have been told that many distinguished Negroes whose careers have brought them South encounter similar difficulties. All the honors in the world cannot buy them a cup of coffee in the lowest greasy-spoon joint. It is not that they crave service in the white man's café over their own——it is simply that in many sparsely settled areas Negro cafés do not exist; and even in densely settled areas, one must sometimes cross town for a glass of water. It is rankling, too, to be encouraged to buy all of one's goods in white stores and then be refused soda-fountain or rest-room service.

No, it makes no sense, but in so far as the Negro is concerned, nothing makes much sense. This was brought home to me in another realm many times when I sought jobs.

The foreman of one plant in Mobile, a large brute, allowed me to tell him what I could do. Then he looked me in the face and spoke to me in these words:

"No, you couldn't get anything like that here."

His voice was not unkind. It was the dead voice one often hears. Determined to see if I could break in somehow, I said: "But if I could do you a better job, and you paid me less than a white man . . ."

"I'll tell you . . . we don't want you people. Don't you understand that?"

"I know," I said with real sadness. "You can't blame a man for trying at least."

"No use trying down here," he said. "We're gradually getting you people weeded out from the better jobs at this plant. We're taking it slow, but we're doing it. Pretty soon we'll have it so the only jobs you can get here are the ones no white man would have."

"How can we live?" I asked hopelessly, careful not to give the impression I was arguing.

"That's the whole point," he said, looking me square in the eyes, but with some faint sympathy, as though he regretted the need to say what followed: "We're going to do our damndest to drive every one of you out of the state."

Despite his frankness and the harshness of his intentions, I nevertheless had the impression he was telling me: "I'm sorry. I've got nothing against you personally, but you're colored, and with all this noise about equality, we just don't want you people around. The only way we can keep you out of our schools and cafés is to make life so hard for you that you'll get the hell out before equality comes."

This attitude cropped up often. Many otherwise decent men and women could find no other solution. They are willing to degrade themselves to their basest levels to prevent the traditional laborer from rising in status or, to put it bluntly, from "winning," even though what he wins has been rightfully his from the moment he was born into the human race.

I walked through the streets of Mobile throughout the afternoons. I had known the city before, in my youth, when I sailed from there once to France. I knew it then as a privileged white. It had impressed me as a beautiful Southern port town, gracious and calm. I had seen the Negro dock workers stripped to the waist, their bodies glistening with sweat under their loads. The sight had chilled me, touched me to pity for men who so resembled beasts of burden. But I had dismissed it as belonging to the natural order of things. The Southern whites I knew were kind and wise. If they allowed this, then surely it must be right.

Now, walking the same streets as a Negro, I found no trace of the Mobile I formerly knew, nothing familiar. The laborers still dragged out their oxlike lives, but the gracious Southerner, the wise Southerner, the kind Southerner was nowhere visible. I knew that if I were white, I would find him easily, for his other face is there for whites to see. It is not a false face; it is simply different from the one the Negro sees. The Negro sees him as a man with muscular emotions who wants to drive out all of his race except the beasts of burden.

I concluded that, as in everything else, the atmosphere of a place is entirely different for Negro and white. The Negro sees and reacts differently not because he is Negro, but because he is suppressed. Fear dims even the sunlight.

▼ ▼ ▼

NOVEMBER 24

I hitchhiked up toward the swamp country between Mobile and Montgomery. A magnificent cool day.

I walked some miles before a large, pleasant-faced man halted his light truck and told me to get in. When I opened the door I saw a shotgun propped against the seat next to his knee. I recalled it was considered sport among some elements in Alabama to hunt "nigs" and I backed away.

"Come on," he laughed. "That's for hunting deer."

I glanced again at his florid face, saw he looked decent and climbed into the leather seat beside him.

"Do you have any luck getting rides through here?" he asked.

"No sir. You're my first ride since Mobile."

I learned he was a married man, fifty-three years old, father of a family now grown and grandfather of two children. He was certainly, by the tone of his conversation, an active civic leader and respected member of his community. I began to hope that I had encountered a decent white.

"You married?" he asked.

"Yes sir."

"Any kids?"

"Yes sir—three."

"You got a pretty wife?"

"Yes sir."

He waited a moment and then with lightness, paternal amusement, "She ever had it from a white man?"

I stared at my black hands, saw the gold wedding band and mumbled something meaningless, hoping he would see my reticence. He overrode my feelings and the conversation grew more salacious. He told me how all of the white men in the region craved colored girls. He said he hired a lot of them both for housework and in his business. "And I guarantee you, I've had it in every one of them before they ever got on the payroll." A pause. Silence above humming tires on the hot-top road. "What do you think of that?"

"Surely some refuse," I suggested cautiously.

"Not if they want to eat—or feed their kids," he snorted. "If they don't put out, they don't get the job."

I looked out the window to tall pine trees rising on either side of the highway. Their turpentine odor mingled with the soaped smells of the man's khaki hunting clothes.

"You think that's pretty terrible, don't you?" he asked.

I knew I should grin and say, "Why no—it's just nature," or some other disarming remark to avoid provoking him.

"Don't you?" he insisted pleasantly.

"I guess I do."

"Why hell—everybody does it. Don't you know that?"

"No sir."

"Well, they sure as hell do. We figure we're doing you people a favor to get some white blood in your kids."

The grotesque hypocrisy slapped me as it does all Negroes. It is worth remembering when the white man talks of the Negro's lack of sexual morality, or when he speaks with horror about mongrelization and with fervor about racial purity. Mongrelization is already a widespread reality in the South—it has been exclusively the white man's contribution to the Southern Way of Life. His vast concern for "racial purity" obviously does not extend to all races.[1]

This aspect of Southern life does not hit the newspapers because, as my companion said, "Alabama nigger women are good about that—they won't never go to the cops or tell on you."

It was obvious what would happen if one of them tried it.

As I feared it would, my lack of "cooperation" nettled the driver. He took my silence, rightly, for disapproval.

"Where you from?" he asked.

"Texas."

"What're you doing down here?"

"Just traveling around, trying to find jobs."

"You're not down here to stir up trouble, are you?"

"Ohgodno."

"You start stirring up these niggers and we sure as hell know how to take care of you."

"I don't intend to."

"Do you know what we do to troublemakers down here?"

"No sir."

"We either ship them off to the pen or kill them."

He spoke in a tone that sickened me, casual, merciless. I looked at him. His decent blue eyes turned yellow. I knew that nothing could touch him to have mercy once he decided a Negro should be "taught a lesson." The immensity of it terrified me. But it caught him up like a lust now. He entertained it, his voice unctuous with pleasure and cruelty. The highway stretched deserted through the swamp forests.

---

[1] Later I encountered many whites who freely admitted the same practices my companion described. In fairness, however, other Southern whites roundly condemned it and claimed it was not as typical as my informants suggested. None denied that it was widespread.

He nodded toward the solid wall of brush flying past our windows.

"You can kill a nigger and toss him into that swamp and no one'll ever know what happened to him."

"Yes sir . . ."

I forced myself to silence, forced myself to picture this man in his other roles. I saw him as he played with his grandchildren, as he stood up in church with open hymnal in hand, as he drank a cup of coffee in the morning before dressing and then shaved and talked with his wife pleasantly about nothing, as he visited with friends on the front porch Sunday afternoons. That was the man I had seen when I first got into the truck. The amiable, decent American was in all his features. This was the dark tangent in every man's belly, the sickness, the coldness, the mercilessness, the lust to cause pain or fear through self-power. Surely not even his wife or closest friends had ever seen him like this. It was a side he would show no one but his victims, or those who connived with him. The rest—what he really must be as a husband, devoted father and respected member of the community—I had to supply with my imagination. He showed me the lowest and I had to surmise the highest.

His face was set hard in an attempt to regain his equilibrium, when he pulled off the main highway and stopped on a dirt road that led into the jungle. We had engaged in a subtle battle of which I think he had only then become aware. He needed to salvage from it something. "This is where I turn off. I guess you want to stick to the highway."

I thanked him for the ride and opened the door. Before I could get out, he spoke again. "I'll tell you how it is here. We'll do business with you people. We'll sure as hell screw your women. Other than that, you're just *completely off the record as far as we're concerned*. And the quicker you people get that through your heads, the better off you'll be."

"Yes, sir . . ." I stepped out and closed the door. He drove down the side road scattering fine gravel behind his wheels. I listened until his truck was out of hearing distance. The heavy air of evening, putrid with swamp rot, smelled fragrant. I walked across the highway, sat on my duffel and waited for another car. None came. The woods issued no sound. I felt strangely safe, isolated, alone in the stillness of dusk turning to night. First stars appeared in darkening skies still pale and the earth's heat escaped upward.

My mouth was dry and my stomach began to ache for food. I realized I had not eaten or had a drink of water all day. Cold surrounded me rapidly. I got up and began to walk along the highway in the darkness. It was better to walk than to freeze. My duffel pulled heavily at my arms and I knew I could not go far without food and rest.

I wondered at the lack of traffic on Alabama highways. No cars passed. My footsteps on the roadside gravel sloughed in echo from the wall of trees and brush.

After a while a light flickered among the foliage. I hurried forward around the curve of highway until I saw it came from an isolated service station at the top of the hill. When I arrived opposite it, I stood for some time across the highway and watched. An elderly white couple sat inside, surrounded by shelves of groceries and auto supplies, by soft drink machines and cigarette dispensers. They looked kind, gentle, and I framed in advance what I should say to allay any fears they might have of a large Negro appearing out of the night, and to convince them that they should sell me food and drink. Perhaps I might even ask them to let me spend the night sleeping on the floor there.

The woman saw me approach past the lighted gasoline lamps. I whistled to give them warning. She met me at the door. I felt an outgush of warm air and heard country music from a radio when she opened. I glanced through the glass to see the man seated in a chair, his ear close to his small radio.

"Pardon me, ma'am," I said, nodding low. "I'm traveling through to Montgomery. I got stranded on the highway and can't seem to get a ride. I wonder if I could buy something to eat and drink?"

She studied me with suspicion, her eyes hard in their wrinkles.

"We're closing up," she said and stepped back to shut the door.

"Please," I pleaded, not needing to feign abjection. "I've been without food and water all day."

I could see her hesitate, her caution and repugnance struggling against instincts of common decency. She obviously wanted to refuse me. She was also undoubtedly afraid not only of me but of having someone drive up for gasoline and see her waiting on me. But I recalled the driver's statement: "We'll do business with you people." I waited. The night was cold, the country lonely. Even animals had to eat and drink.

"Well, I guess it's all right," she said with disgust. She turned back into the room. I stepped inside and closed the door. Neither of them spoke. The old man glanced up at me from a lean, seamed face devoid of all expression.

I bought an orange drink and a package of cracker sandwiches. The atmosphere was so unhospitable I stepped outside where they could watch me and I drank the orange. When I finished, I returned the empty bottle and quickly bought another. The store had little to offer in the way of food that I could manage. The only two cans of sardines had no keys and the owner stared at the floor, nodding no when I asked if he had a can opener. I bought a fried pie, a loaf of bread and five Milky Way bars.

The woman stood in front of the gas heater and picked the dirt from under her thumbnail with the third finger of her other hand. When I mumbled my thanks, she was so absorbed in her task that she acknowledged my departure only by staring at her hands with a deeper frown. The husband stuck the money in his shirt pocket.

I walked down the highway into the darkness again, carrying both duffel bags in my left hand and feeding myself the tasteless pineapple fried pie with my right.

A distant hum behind me caught my attention. I turned to see a yellow glow on the road's horizon. It grew stronger and headlights appeared. Though I dreaded riding with another white man, I dreaded more staying on the road all night. Stepping out into full view, I waved my arms. An ancient car braked to a halt and I hurried to it. To my great relief, the reflections from the dash light showed me the face of a young Negro man.

We discussed my problem. He said he lived back in the woods, but had six kids and only two rooms. He wouldn't even have a bed to offer me. I asked him about some other house in the area where I might rent a bed. He said there were none any better than what he had to offer.

However, we could find no other solution.

"You can't stand out here all night. If you don't mind sleeping on the floor, you're welcome to come with me," he said finally.

"I don't mind sleeping on the floor," I said. "I just wouldn't want to put you to any trouble."

As we drove several miles down a lane into the forest, he told me he was a sawmill worker and never made quite enough to get out from under his debts. Always, when he took his check to the store, he owed a little more than the check could cover. He said it was the same for everyone else; and indeed I have seen the pattern throughout my travels. Part of the Southern white's strategy is to get the Negro in debt and keep him there.

"It makes it hard, doesn't it?" I said.

"Yeah, but you can't stop," he answered quickly. "That's what I tell the men at the mill. Some of them are willing just to sit there. I told them, 'Okay, so you're going to give up just because you get no butter with your bread. That's no way to act. Go ahead and eat the bread—but work, and maybe someday we'll have butter to go with it.' I tell them we sure ain't going to get it any other way."

I asked him if he could not get together with some of the others and strike for better wages. He laughed with real amusement.

"Do you know how long we'd last, doing something like that?"

"Well, if you stuck together, they sure couldn't kill you all."

"They could damn sure try," he snorted. "Anyway, how long could I feed my kids? There's only a couple of stores in twenty miles. They'd cut off credit and refuse to sell to us. Without money coming in, none of us could live."

He turned off the lane into a rutted path that led through dense underbrush up to a knoll. The headlights fell on a shanty of unpainted wood, patched at the bottom with a rusting Dr. Pepper sign. Except for the voices of children, a deep silence hung over the place. The man's wife came to the door and stood silhouetted against the pale light of a kerosene lamp. He introduced us. Though she appeared embarrassed, she asked me in.

The subdued babble of children mounted to excited shouts of welcome. They ranged in age from nine years to four months. They were overjoyed to have company. It must be a party. We decided it was.

Supper was on the makeshift table. It consisted entirely of large yellow beans cooked in water. The mother prepared mashed beans and canned milk for the infant. I remembered the bread and offered it as my contribution to the meal. Neither parent apologized for the meagerness of the food. We served ourselves on plastic dishes from the table and sat where we could find places, the children on the floor with a spread-out newspaper for a tablecloth.

I congratulated them on such a fine family. The mother told me they had been truly blessed. "Ours are all in good health. When you think of so many people with crippled or blind or not-right children, you just have to thank God." I praised the children until the father's tired face animated with pride. He looked at the children the way another looks at some rare painting or treasured gem.

Closed into the two rooms, with only the soft light of two kerosene lamps, the atmosphere changed. The outside world, outside standards disappeared. They were somewhere beyond in the vast darkness. In here, we had all we needed for gaiety. We had shelter, some food in our bellies, the bodies and eyes and affections of children who were not yet aware of how things were. And we had treats. We cut the Milky Way bars into thin slices for dessert. In a framework of nothing, slices of Milky Way become a great gift. With almost rabid delight, the children consumed them. One of the smaller girls salivated so heavily the chocolate dribbled syruplike from the corner of her mouth. Her mother wiped it off with her fingertip and unconsciously (from what yearning?) put it in her own mouth.

After supper, I went outside with my host to help him carry water from a makeshift boarded well. A near full moon shone above the trees and chill penetrated as though brilliance strengthened it. We picked our way carefully through fear of snakes down a faint footpath to the edge of the trees to urinate. The moon-speckled landscape exhaled

its night rustlings, its truffle-odor of swamps. Distantly the
baby cried. I listened to the muffled rattle of our waters
against damp leaf loam. A fragment of memory returned—
recollection of myself as a youngster reading Lillian Smith's
Strange Fruit, her description of the Negro boy stopping
along a lonely path to urinate. Now, years later, I was
there in a role foreign to my youth's wildest imaginings. I
felt more profoundly than ever before the totality of my
Negro-ness, the immensity of its isolating effects. The
transition was complete from the white boy reading a book
about Negroes in the safety of his white living room to an
old Negro man in the Alabama swamps, his existence nullified by men but reaffirmed by nature, in his functions, in
his affection.

"Okay?" my friend said as we turned back. Moonlight
caught his protruding cheekbones and cast the hollows beneath into shadow.

"Okay," I said.

The house stood above us, rickety, a faint light at the
windows. I could hear the whites say, "Look at that shanty.
They live like animals. If they wanted to do better they
could. And they expect us just to accept them? They *like*
to live this way. It would make them just as miserable to
demand a higher standard of living as it would make us
miserable to put us down to that standard."

I mentioned this to my host. "But we can't do any
better," he said. "We work just for that . . . to have something a little better for the kids and us."

"Your wife doesn't seem to get down in the dumps," I
remarked.

"No—she's good all the way through. I'll tell you—if we
don't have meat to cook with the beans, why she just goes
ahead and cooks the beans anyhow." He said this last with
a flourish that indicated the grandness of her attitude.

We placed buckets of water on the cast-iron wood stove
in the kitchen so we could have warm water for washing
and shaving. Then we returned outside to fill the wood-box.

"Are there really a lot of alligators in these swamps?"
I asked.

"Oh God yes, the place is alive with them."

"Why don't you kill some of them? The tails make good

meat. I could show you how. We learned in jungle training when I was in the army."

"Oh, we can't do that," he said. "They stick a hundred-dollar fine on you for killing a gator. I'm telling you," he laughed sourly, "they got all the loopholes plugged. There ain't a way you can win in this state."

"But what about the children?" I asked. "Aren't you afraid the gators might eat one of them?"

"No . . . he said forlornly, "the gators like turtle better than they do us."

"They must be part white," I heard myself say.

His laughter sounded flat in the cold air. "As long as they keep their bellies full with turtles, they're no danger to us. Anyway, we keep the kids close to the house." [1]

The cheerful and fretful noises of children being readied for bed drifted to us as we returned to the kitchen. Physical modesty in such cramped quarters was impossible, indeed in such a context it would have been ridiculous. The mother sponge-bathed the children while the husband and I shaved. Each of the children went to the toilet, a zinc bucket in the corner, since it was too cold for them to go outside.

Their courtesy to me was exquisite. While we spread tow sacks on the floor and then feed sacks over them, the children asked questions about my own children. Did they go to school? No, they were too young. How old were they then? Why, today is my daughter's fifth birthday. Would she have a party? Yes, she'd certainly had a party. Excitement. Like we had here, with the candy and everything? Yes, something like that.

But it was time to go to bed, time to stop asking questions. The magic remained for them, almost unbearable to me—the magic of children thrilled to know my daughter had a party. The parents brought in patchwork quilts from under the bed in the other room and spread them over the pallets. The children kissed their parents and then wanted to kiss Mr. Griffin. I sat down on a straight-back kitchen chair and held out my arms. One by one they came, smelling of soap and childhood. One by one they put their arms

---

[1] The fine for killing alligators appears to be a conservation measure and means of controlling turtles, not a punitive action against the Negroes, though few Negroes realize this.

around my neck and touched their lips to mine. One by one they said and giggled soberly, "Good night, Mr. Griffin."

I stepped over them to go to my pallet near the kitchen door and lay down fully dressed. Warning the children he did not want to hear another word from them, the father picked up the kerosene lamp and carried it into the bedroom. Through the doorless opening I saw light flicker on the walls. Neither of them spoke. I heard the sounds of undressing. The lamp was blown out and a moment later their bedspring creaked.

Fatigue spread through me, making me grateful for the tow-sack bed. I fought back glimpses of my daughter's birthday party in its cruel contrasts to our party here tonight.

"If you need anything, Mr. Griffin, just holler," the man said.

"Thank you. I will. Good night."

"Good night," the children said, their voices locating them in the darkness.

"Good night," again.

"Good night, Mr. Griffin."

"That's enough," the father called out warningly to them.

I lay there watching moonlight pour through the crack of the ill-fitting door as everyone drifted to sleep. Mosquitoes droned loudly until the room was a great hum. I wondered that they should be out on such a cold night. The children jerked in their sleep and I knew they had been bitten. The stove cooled gradually with almost imperceptible interior pops and puffings. Odors of the night and autumn and the swamp entered to mingle with the inside odors of children, kerosene, cold beans, urine and the dead incense of pine ashes. The rots and the freshness combined into a strange fragrance—the smell of poverty. For a moment I knew the intimate and subtle joys of misery.

And yet misery was the burden, the pervading, killing burden. I understood why they had so many children. These moments of night when the swamp and darkness surrounded them evoked an immense loneliness, a dread, a sense of exile from the rest of humanity. When the awareness of it strikes, a man either suffocates with despair or he turns to cling to his woman, to console and seek consolation. Their union is momentary escape from the swamp night, from utter hopelessness of its ever getting better for them. It is an ultimately tragic act wherein the hopeless seek hope.

Thinking about these things, the bravery of these people attempting to bring up a family decently, their gratitude that none of their children were blind or maimed, their willingness to share their food and shelter with a stranger—the whole thing overwhelmed me. I got up from bed, half-frozen anyway, and stepped outside.

A thin fog blurred the moon. Trees rose as ghostly masses in the diffused light. I sat on an inverted washtub and trembled as its metallic coldness seeped through my pants.

I thought of my daughter, Susie, and of her fifth birthday today, the candles, the cake and party dress; and of my sons in their best suits. They slept now in clean beds in a warm house while their father, a bald-headed old Negro, sat in the swamps and wept, holding it in so he would not awaken the Negro children.

I felt again the Negro children's lips soft against mine, so like the feel of my own children's good-night kisses. I saw again their large eyes, guileless, not yet aware that doors into wonderlands of security, opportunity and hope were closed to them.

It was thrown in my face. I saw it not as a white man and not as a Negro, but as a human parent. Their children resembled mine in all ways except the superficial one of skin color, as indeed they resembled all children of all humans. Yet this accident, this least important of all qualities, the skin pigment, marked them for inferior status. It became fully terrifying when I realized that if my skin were permanently black, they would unhesitatingly consign my own children to this bean future.

One can scarcely conceive the full horror of it unless one is a parent who takes a close look at his children and then asks himself how he would feel if a group of men should come to his door and tell him they had decided—for reasons of convenience to them—that his children's lives would henceforth be restricted, their world smaller, their educational opportunities less, their future mutilated.

One would then see it as the Negro parent sees it, for this is precisely what happens. He looks at his children and knows. No one, not even a saint, can live without a sense of personal value. The white racist has masterfully defrauded the Negro of this sense. It is the least obvious but most heinous of all race crimes, for it kills the spirit and the will to live.

It was too much. Though I was experiencing it, I could not believe it. Surely in America a whole segment of decent souls could not stand by and allow such massive crimes to be committed. I tried to see the whites' side, as I have all along. I have studied objectively the anthropological arguments, the accepted clichés about cultural and ethnic differences. And I have found their application simply untrue. The two great arguments—the Negro's lack of sexual morality and his intellectual incapacity—are smoke screens to justify prejudice and unethical behavior. Recent scientific studies, published in *The Eighth Generation* (Harper & Brothers, New York), show that the contemporary middle-class Negro has the same family cult, the same ideals and goals as his white counterpart. The Negro's lower scholastic showing springs not from racial default, but from being deprived of cultural and educational advantages by the whites. When the segregationist argues that the Negro is scholastically inferior, he presents the most eloquent possible argument for desegregated schools; he admits that so long as the Negro is kept in tenth-rate schools he will remain scholastically behind white children.

I have held no brief for the Negro. I have looked diligently for all aspects of "inferiority" among them and I cannot find them. All the cherished question-begging epithets applied to the Negro race, and widely accepted as truth even by men of good will, simply prove untrue when one lives among them. This, of course, excludes the trash element, which is the same everywhere and is no more evident among Negroes than whites.

When all the talk, all the propaganda has been cut away, the criterion is nothing but the color of skin. My experience proved that. They judged me by no other quality. My skin was dark. That was sufficient reason for them to deny me those rights and freedoms without which life loses its significance and becomes a matter of little more than animal survival.

I searched for some other answer and found none. I had spent a day without food and water for no other reason than that my skin was black. I was sitting on a tub in the swamp for no other reason.

I went back into the shanty. The air was slightly warmer and smelled of kerosene, tow sacks and humanity. I lay down in the darkness, in the midst of snores.

"Mr. Griffin . . . Mr. Griffin."

I heard the man's soft voice above my shouts. I awakened to see the kerosene lamp and beyond it my host's troubled face.

"Are you all right?" he asked. In the surrounding darkness I sensed the tension. They lay silent, not snoring.

"I'm sorry," I said. "I was having a nightmare."

He stood upright. From my position flat on the floor his head appeared to touch the ceiling beams far above. "Are you all right now?"

"Yes, thank you for waking me up."

He stepped carefully over the children and returned to the other room.

It was the same nightmare I had been having recently. White men and women, their faces stern and heartless, closed in on me. The hate stare burned through me. I pressed back against a wall. I could expect no pity, no mercy. They approached slowly and I could not escape them. Twice before, I had awakened myself screaming.

I listened for the family to settle back into sleep. The mosquitoes swarmed. I lighted a cigarette, hoping its smoke would drive them out.

The nightmare worried me. I had begun this experiment in a spirit of scientific detachment. I wanted to keep my feelings out of it, to be objective in my observations. But it was becoming such a profound personal experience, it haunted even my dreams.

My host called me again at dawn. His wife stood in lamplight at the stove, pouring coffee. I washed my face in a bowl of water she had heated for me. We spoke by nods and smiles to avoid waking the children sprawled on the floor.

After breakfast of coffee and a slice of bread, we were ready to leave. I shook hands with her at the door and thanked her. Reaching for my wallet, I told her I wanted to pay her for putting me up.

She refused, saying that I had brought more than I had taken. "If you gave us a penny, we'd owe you change."

I left money with her as a gift for the children, and the husband drove me back to the highway.

The morning was bright and cool. Before long a car with two young white boys picked me up. I quickly saw that they were, like many of their generation, kinder than the older ones. They drove me to a small-town bus station where I could catch a bus.

I bought a ticket to Montgomery and went to sit outside on the curb where other Negro passengers gathered. Many Negroes walked through the streets. Their glances were kind and communicative, as though all of us shared some common secret.

As I sat in the sunlight, a great heaviness came over me. I went inside to the Negro rest room, splashed cold water on my face and brushed my teeth. Then I brought out my hand mirror and inspected myself. I had been a Negro more than three weeks and it no longer shocked me to see the stranger in the mirror. My hair had grown to a heavy fuzz, my face skin, with the continued medication, exposure to sunlight and ground-in stain, was what Negroes call a "pure brown"—a smooth dark color that made me look like millions of others.

I noted, too, that my face had lost animation. In repose, it had taken on the strained, disconsolate expression that is written on the countenance of so many Southern Negroes. My mind had become the same way, dozing empty for long periods. It thought of food and water, but so many hours were spent just waiting, cushioning self against dread, that it no longer thought of much else. Like the others in my condition, I was finding life too burdensome.

I felt a great hunger for something merely pleasurable, for something people call "fun." The need was so great that deep within, through the squalor and the humiliations of this life, I took some joy in the mere fact that I could be alone for a while inside the rest-room cubicle with its clean plumbing and unfinished wood walls. Here I had a water faucet to drink from and I could experience the luxury of splashing cold water on my face as much as I wanted. Here, with a latch on the door, I was isolated from the hate stares, the contempt.

The smell of Ivory livened the atmosphere. Some of the stain came off and I wondered how long it would be before I could pass as white again. I decided to take no more pills for a while. I removed my shirt and undershirt. My body, so long unexposed to the sun or the sun lamp, had paled to a *café-au-lait* color. I told myself I would have to be careful not to undress unless I had privacy henceforth. My face and hands were far darker than my body. Since I often slept in my clothes, the problem would not be great.

I wet my sponge, poured dye on it and touched up the corners of my mouth and my lips, which were always the difficult spots.

We boarded the bus in late afternoon and rode without incident to Selma, where I had a long layover before taking another bus into the state capital.

In deep dusk I strolled through the streets of the beautiful town. A group of nicely dressed Negro women solicited contributions for missionary activities. I placed some change in their cup and accepted a tract explaining the missionary program. Then, curious to see how they would fare with the whites, I walked along with them.

We approached the stationkeeper. His face soured and he growled his refusal. We walked on. In not a single instance did a white hear them out.

Two well-dressed men stood talking in front of the Hotel Albert.

"Pardon us, sir," one of the women said, holding a tract in her hand. "We're soliciting contributions for our missionary——"

"G'wan," the older one snapped, "I got too many of them damned tracts already."

The younger man hesitated, dug in his pocket and tossed a handful of change into the cup. He refused the tract, saying, "I'm sure the money'll be put to good use."

After we had gone two blocks, we heard footsteps behind us. We stopped at a street corner, not looking back. The younger man's voice came to us. "I don't suppose it does any good," he said quietly, "but I apologize for the bad manners of my people."

"Thank you," we said, not turning our heads.

As we passed the bus station, I dropped out of the little group and sat on a public bench near an outside phone booth. I waited until I saw a Negro use the phone, and then I hurried to it, closed the door and asked the long-distance operator to call my home collect.

When my wife answered, the strangeness of my situation again swept over me. I talked with her and the children as their husband and father, while reflected in the glass windows of the booth I saw another man they would not know. At this time, when I wanted most to lose the illusion, I was more than ever aware of it, aware that it was not the man she knew, but a stranger who spoke with the same voice and had the same memory.

Happy at least to have heard their voices, I stepped from the booth to the night's cooler air. The night was always a comfort. Most of the whites were in their homes. The threat was less. A Negro blended inconspicuously into the darkness.

> *Night coming tenderly*
> *Black like me.*

At such a time, the Negro can look at the starlit skies and find that he has, after all, a place in the universal order of things. The stars, the black skies affirm his humanity, his validity as a human being. He knows that his belly, his lungs, his tired legs, his appetites, his prayers and his mind are cherished in some profound involvement with nature and God. The night is his consolation. It does not despise him.

The roar of wheels turning into the station, the stench of exhaust fumes, the sudden bustle of people unloading told me it was time to go. Men, better and wiser than the night, put me back into my place with their hate stares.

I walked to the back of the bus, past the drowsers, and found an empty seat. The Negroes gave me their sleepy smiles and then we were off. I leaned back and dozed along with the others.

▼ ▼ ▼

NOVEMBER 25

In Montgomery, the capital of Alabama, I encountered a new atmosphere. The Negro's feeling of utter hopelessness is here replaced by a determined spirit of passive resistance. The Reverend Martin Luther King, Jr.'s influence, like an echo of Gandhi's, prevails. Nonviolent and prayerful resistance to discrimination is the keynote. Here, the Negro has committed himself to a definite stand. He will go to jail, suffer any humiliation, but he will not back down. He will take the insults and abuses stoically so that his children will not have to take them in the future.

The white racist is bewildered and angered by such an attitude, because the dignity of the Negro's course of action emphasizes the indignity of his own. It is a challenge to him to needle the Negro into acts of a baser nature, into open physical conflict. He will walk up and blow cigarette smoke in the Negro's face, hoping the Negro will strike out at him. Then he could repress the Negro violently and claim it was only self-defense.

Where the Negro has lacked unity of purpose elsewhere, he has in Montgomery rallied to the leadership of King. Where he has been degraded elsewhere by unjust men of both races, here he is resisting degradation.

I could not make out the white viewpoint in Montgomery. It was too fluid, too changeable. A superficial calm hung over the city. At night police were everywhere. I felt that the two races stood like blocks of concrete, immovable, and that the basic issues of right and wrong, of justice and injustice, were lost from view by the whites. The issues had degenerated to who would win. Fear and dread tensed both sides.

The Negroes with whom I associated feared two things. They feared that one of their own might commit an act of violence that would jeopardize their position by allowing the whites to say they were too dangerous to have their rights. They dreaded the awful tauntings of irresponsible white men, the jailing, the frames.

The white man's fears have been widely broadcast. To the Negro these fears of "intermingling" make no sense. All he can see is that the white man wants to hold him down—to make him live up to his responsibilities as a taxpayer and soldier, while denying him the privileges of a citizen. At base, though the white brings forth many arguments to justify his viewpoint, one feels the reality is simply that he cannot bear to "lose" to the traditionally servant class.

The hate stare was everywhere practiced, especially by women of the older generation. On Sunday, I made the experiment of dressing well and walking past some of the white churches just as services were over. In each instance, as the women came through the church doors and saw me, the "spiritual bouquets" changed to hostility. The transformation was grotesque. In all of Montgomery only one woman refrained. She did not smile. She merely looked at me and did not change her expression. My gratitude to her was so great it astonished me.

▼ ▼ ▼

NOVEMBER 27

I remained in my room more and more each day. The situation in Montgomery was so strange I decided to try passing back into white society. I went out only at night for food. My heart sickened at the thought of any more hate. Too, I wanted no more sunlight until I had the medication sufficiently out of my system to allow me to lighten.

NOVEMBER 28

I decided to try to pass back into white society. I scrubbed myself almost raw until my brown skin had a pink rather than black undertone. Yes, looking into the mirror, I felt I could pass. I put on a white shirt, but by contrast it made my face and hands appear too dark. I changed to a brown sports shirt which made my skin appear lighter.

This shift was nerve-racking. As a white man I could not be seen leaving a Negro home at midnight. If I checked into a white hotel and then got too much sun, it would, in combination with the medication still in my system, turn me too dark and I would not be able to return to the hotel.

I waited until the streets were quiet outside and I was sure everyone in the house slept. Then, taking my bags, I walked to the door and out into the night.

It was important to get out of the neighborhood and into the white sector as quickly and inconspicuously as possible. I watched for police cars. Only one appeared in the distance and I dodged down a side street.

At the next intersection a Negro teen-ager strode by. I stepped out and walked behind him. He glanced at me and then kept his eyes to the front. Obviously thinking I might harass him, he pulled something from his jacket and I heard a click. Though I could not see what he held in his hand, I have no doubt it was a switch-blade knife. To him I was nothing more than a white stranger, a potential source of harm against whom he must protect himself.

He stopped at the corner of a wide street and waited to cross. I came up beside him.

"It's getting cold, isn't it?" I said, seeking to reassure him that I had no unfriendly intentions.

He stood like a statue, unresponsive.

We crossed the street into a brighter downtown section. A policeman strolled toward us and the boy quickly dropped his weapon into his jacket pocket.

The policeman nodded affably to me and I knew then that I had successfully passed back into white society, that I was once more a first-class citizen, that all doors into cafés, rest rooms, libraries, movies, concerts, schools and churches were suddenly open to me. After so long I could not adjust to it. A sense of exultant liberation flooded through me. I crossed over to a restaurant and entered. I took a seat beside white men at the counter and the waitress smiled at me. It was a miracle. I ordered food and was served, and it was a miracle. I went to the rest room and was not molested. No one paid me the slightest attention. No one said, "What're you doing in here, nigger?"

Out there in the night I knew that men who were exactly as I had been these past weeks roamed the streets and not one of them could go into a place and buy a cup of coffee at this time of the night. Instead of opening the door into rest rooms, they looked for alleys.

To them as to me, these simple privileges would be a miracle. But though I felt it all, I felt no joy in it. I saw smiles, benign faces, courtesies—a side of the white man I had not seen in weeks, but I remembered too well the other side. The miracle was sour.

I ate the white meal, drank the white water, received the white smiles and wondered how it could all be. What sense could a man make of it?

I left the café and walked to the elegant Whitney Hotel. A Negro rushed to take my knapsacks. He gave me the smiles, the "yes, sir—yes, sir."

I felt like saying, "You're not fooling me," but now I was back on the other side of the wall. There was no longer communication between us, no longer the glance that said everything.

The white clerks registered me, surrounded me with

smiles, sent me to my comfortable room accompanied by
a Negro who carried my bags. I gave him his tip, received
his bow and realized that already he was far from me, distant as the Negro is distant from the white. I locked the
door, sat on the bed and smoked a cigarette. I was the
same man who could not possibly have bought his way
into this room a week ago. My inclination was to marvel
at the feel of the carpet beneath my feet, to catalogue the
banal miracle of every stick of furniture, every lamp, the
telephone, to go and wash myself in the tile shower—or
again to go out into the street simply to experience what
it was like to walk into all the doors, all the joints and
movies and restaurants, to talk to white men in the lobby
without servility, to look at women and see them smile
courteously.

▼ ▼ ▼

NOVEMBER 29

Montgomery looked different that morning. The face of
humanity smiled—good smiles, full of warmth; irresistible
smiles that confirmed my impression that these people were
simply unaware of the situation with the Negroes who
passed them on the street—that there was not even the
communication of intelligent awareness between them. I
talked with some—casual conversations here and there.
They said they knew the Negroes, they had had long talks
with the Negroes. They did not know that the Negro long
ago learned he must tell them what they want to hear, not
what is. I heard the old things: the Negro is this or that or
the other. You have to go slow. You can't expect the
South to sit back and let the damned communist North
dictate to it, especially when no outsider can really "understand." I listened and kept my tongue from giving answer.
This was the time to listen, not to talk, but it was difficult.
I looked into their eyes and saw sincerity and wanted to

say: "Don't you know you are prattling the racist poison?"

Montgomery, the city I had detested, was beautiful that day; at least it was until I walked into a Negro section where I had not been before. I was a lone white man in a Negro neighborhood. I, the white man, got from the Negro the same shriveling treatment I, the Negro, had got from the white man. I thought, "Why me? I have been one of you." Then I realized it was the same stupidity I had encountered at the New Orleans bus station. It was nothing I had done, it was not me, but the color of my skin. Their looks said: "You white bastard, you ofay sonofabitch, what are you doing walking these streets?" just as the whites' looks had said a few days before: "You black bastard, you nigger sonofabitch, what are you doing walking these streets?"

Was it worth going on? Was it worth trying to show the one race what went on behind the mask of the other?

▼ ▼ ▼

DECEMBER 1

I developed a technique of zigzagging back and forth. In my bag I kept a damp sponge, dyes, cleansing cream and Kleenex. It was hazardous, but it was the only way to traverse an area both as Negro and white. As I traveled, I would find an isolated spot, perhaps an alley at night or the brush beside a highway, and quickly apply the dye to face, hands and legs, then rub off and reapply until it was firmly anchored in my pores. I would go through the area as a Negro and then, usually at night, remove the dyes with cleansing cream and tissues and pass through the same area as a white man.

I was the same man, whether white or black. Yet when I was white, I received the brotherly-love smiles and the privileges from whites and the hate stares or obsequiousness from the Negroes. And when I was a Negro, the whites

judged me fit for the junk heap, while the Negroes treated
me with great warmth.

As the Negro Griffin, I walked up the steep hill to the
bus station in Montgomery to get the schedule for buses to
Tuskegee. I received the information from a polite clerk
and turned away from the counter.

"Boy!" I heard a woman's voice, harsh and loud.

I glanced toward the door to see a large, matriarchical
woman, elderly and impatient. Her pinched face grimaced
and she waved me to her.

"Boy, come here. Hurry!"

Astonished, I obeyed.

"Get those bags out of the cab," she ordered testily,
seeming outraged with my lack of speed.

Without thinking, I allowed my face to spread to a grin
as though overjoyed to serve her. I carried her bags to the
bus and received three haughty dimes. I thanked her profusely. Her eyebrows knitted with irritation and she finally
waved me away.

I took the early afternoon bus for Tuskegee, walked
through a Southern town of great beauty and tranquility.
The famed Tuskegee Institute was, I learned, out of the
city limits. In fact the major portion of the Negro residential area is out of the city limits—put there when the city
fathers decided it was the simplest way to invalidate the
Negro vote in local elections.

The spirit of George Washington Carver hangs strongly
over the campus—a quiet, almost hauntingly quiet area of
trees and grass. It radiates an atmosphere of respect for
the work of one's hands and mind, of human dignity. In
interviews here, my previous findings were confirmed: with
the exception of those trained in professions where they
can set up independent practice, they can find jobs commensurate with their education only outside the South. I
found an atmosphere of great courtesy, with students more
dignified and more soberly dressed than one finds on most
white campuses. Education for them is a serious business.
They are so close to the days when their ancestors were
kept totally illiterate, when their ancestors learned to read
and write at the risk of severe punishment, that learning is

an almost sacred privilege now. They see it also as the only possible way out of the morass in which the Negro finds himself.

Later that afternoon, after wandering around the town, I turned back toward the Institute to talk with the dean. A white man stood in front of a Negro recreation parlor near the college entrance gates and waved to me. I hesitated at first, fearing he would be just another bully. But his eyes pleaded with me to trust him.

I crossed slowly over to him.

"Did you want me?" I asked.

"Yes—could you tell me where is Tuskegee Institute?"

"Right there," I said, pointing to the gates a block away.

"Aw, I know it," he grinned. I smelled whisky in the fresh evening air. "I was just looking for an excuse to talk to you," he admitted. "Do you teach here?"

"No, I'm just traveling through," I said.

"I'm a Ph.D.," he said uncomfortably. "I'm from New York—down here as an observer."

"For some government agency?"

"No, strictly on my own," he said. I studied him closely, since other Negroes were beginning to watch us. He appeared to be in his early fifties and was well enough dressed.

"How about you and me having a drink?" he said.

"No, thanks," I said and turned away.

"Wait a minute, dammit. You people are my brothers. It's people like me that are your only hope. How do you expect me to observe if you won't talk to me?"

"Very well," I said. "I'll be glad to talk with you."

"Hell, I've observed all I can stomach," he said. "Let's us go get just roaring blinko drunk and forget all this damned prejudice stuff."

"A white man and a Negro," I laughed. "We'd both hear from the merciful Klan."

"Damned right—a white man and a Negro. Hell, I don't consider myself any better than you—not even as good, maybe. I'm just trying to show some brotherhood."

Though I knew he had been drinking, I wondered that an educated man and an observer could be so obtuse—could create such an embarrassing situation for a Negro.

"I appreciate it," I said stiffly. "But it would never work."

"They needn't know," he whispered, leaning close to me, an almost frantic look in his eyes as though he were begging not to be rejected. "I'm going to get soused anyway. Hell, I've had all this I can stand. It's just between you and me. We could go into the woods somewhere. Come on—for brotherhood's sake."

I felt great pity for him. He was obviously lonely and fearful of rejection by the very people he sought to help. But I wondered if he could know how offensive this overweaning "brotherhood" demonstration was. Others stood by and watched with frowns of disapproval.

At that moment a Negro drove up in an old car and stopped. Ignoring the white man, he spoke to me. "Would you like to buy some nice fat turkeys?" he asked.

"I don't have any family here," I said.

"Wait a minute there," the white man said. "Hell, I'll buy all your turkeys . . . just to help you out. I'll show you fellows that not all white men are bastards. How many've you got in there?" We looked into the car and saw several live turkeys in the back seat.

"How much for all of them?" the white man asked, pulling a ten-dollar bill from his wallet.

The vendor looked at me, puzzled, as though he did not wish to unload such a baggage on the generous white man.

"What can you do with them when you get them out of the car?" I asked.

"What're you trying to do," the white man asked belligerently, "kill this man's sale?"

The vendor quickly put in: "No . . . no, mister, he's not trying to do that. I'm glad to sell you all the turkeys you want. But where you want me to unload them? You live around here?"

"No, I'm just an observer. Hell, take the ten dollars. I'll give the damned turkeys away."

When the vendor hesitated, the white man asked: "What's the matter—did you steal them or something?"

"Oh, no sir . . ."

"You afraid I'm a cop or something?"

The unpardonable had been said. The white man, despite his protestations of brotherhood, had made the first dirty suggestion that came to his mind. He was probably unaware of it but it escaped none of us. By the very tone of his question he revealed his contempt for us. His voice had taken on a hard edge, putting us in our place, as they say. He had become just like the whites he decried.

"I didn't steal them," the turkey man said coldly. "You can come out to my farm. I've got more there."

The white man, sensing the change, the resentment, glared at me. "Hell, no wonder nobody has any use for you. You don't give a man a chance to be nice to you. And damn it, I'm going to put that in my report." He turned away grumbling. "There's something 'funny' about all of you." Then he raised his head toward the evening sky and announced furiously: "But before I do anything else, I'm going to get drunk, stinking drunk."

He stamped off down the road toward open country. Negroes around me shook their heads slowly, with regret. We had witnessed a pitiful one-man attempt to make up for some of the abuses the man had seen practiced against the Negro. It had failed miserably. If I had dared, I would have gone after him and tried to bridge the terrible gap that had come between him and us.

Instead, I walked to the street lamp and wrote in my notebook.

"We must return to them their lawful rights, assure equality of justice—and then everybody leave everybody else to hell alone. Paternalistic—we show our prejudice in our paternalism—we downgrade their dignity."

It was too late to visit the dean of Tuskegee, so I went to the bus station and boarded a bus for Atlanta, via Auburn, Alabama.

The trip was without incident until we changed buses at Auburn. As always, we Negroes sat at the rear. Four of us occupied the back bench. A large, middle-aged Negro woman sat in front of us to the left, a young Negro man occupied the seat in front of us to the right.

At one of the stops, two white women boarded and could find no place to sit. No gallant Southern white man (or youth) rose to offer them a place in the "white section."

The bus driver called back and asked the young Negro man and the middle-aged Negro woman to sit together so the white women could have one of the seats. Both ignored the request. We felt the tensions mount as whites craned to stare back at us.

A redheaded white man in a sports shirt stood up, faced the rear and called out to the Negro. "Didn't you hear the driver? Move out, man."

"They're welcome to sit here," the Negro said quietly, indicating the empty seat beside him and the one beside the woman across the aisle.

The driver looked dumfounded and then dismayed. He walked halfway to the rear and, struggling to keep his voice under control, said: "They don't want to sit with you people, don't you know that? They don't want to—is that plain enough?"

We felt an incident boiling, but none of us wanted the young Negro, who had paid for his ticket, to be forced to vacate his seat. If the women did not want to sit with us, then let one of the white men offer his seat and he could come and sit with us. The young Negro said no more. He gazed out the window.

The redhead bristled. "Do you want me to slap these two jigaboos out of their seats?" he asked the driver in a loud voice.

We winced and turned into mummies, staring vacantly, insulating ourselves against further insults.

"No—for God's sake—please—no rough stuff," the driver pleaded.

One of the white women looked toward us apologetically, as though she were sorry to be the cause of such a scene. "It's all right," she said. "Please . . ." asking the driver and the young man to end their attempts to get her a seat.

The redhead flexed his chest muscles and slowly took his seat, glaring back at us. A young teen-ager, sitting halfway to the front, sniggered: "Man, he was going to slap that nigger, all right." The white bully was his hero, but other whites maintained a disapproving silence.

At the Atlanta station we waited for the whites to get off. One of them, a large middle-aged man, hesitated, turned and stepped back toward us. We hardened ourselves for another insult. He bent over to speak to the young Negro. "I just wanted to tell you that before he slapped you, he'd have had to slap me down first," he said.

None of us smiled. We wondered why he had not spoken up while whites were still on the bus. We nodded our appreciation and the young Negro said gently: "It happens to us all the time."

"Well, I just wanted you to know—I was on your side, boy." He winked, never realizing how he had revealed himself to us by calling our companion by the hated name of "boy." We nodded wearily in response to his parting nod.

I was the last to leave the bus. An elderly white man, bald and square of build, dressed in worn blue work clothes, peered intently at me. Then he crimped his face as though I were odious and snorted, "Phew!" His small blue eyes shone with repugnance, a look of such unreasoning contempt for my skin that it filled me with despair.

It was a little thing, but piled on all the other little things it broke something in me. Suddenly I had had enough. Suddenly I could stomach no more of this degradation—not of myself but of all men who were black like me. Abruptly I turned and walked away. The large bus station was crowded with humanity. In the men's room, I entered one of the cubicles and locked the door. For a time I was safe, isolated; for a time I owned the space around me, though it was scarcely more than that of a coffin. In medieval times, men sought sanctuary in churches. Nowadays, for a nickel, I could find sanctuary in a colored rest room. Then, sanctuary had the smell of incense-permeated walls. Now it had the odor of disinfectant.

The irony of it hit me. I was back in the land of my forefathers, Georgia. The town of Griffin was named for one of them. Too I, a Negro, carried the name hated by all Negroes, for former Governor Griffin (no kin that I would care to discover) devoted himself heroically to the task of keeping Negroes "in their place." Thanks in part to his efforts, this John Griffin celebrated a triumphant return to the land from which his people had sprung by seeking sanctuary in a toilet cubicle at the bus station.

I took out my cleansing cream and rubbed it on my hands and face to remove the stain. I then removed my shirt and undershirt, rubbed my skin almost raw with the undershirt, and looked into my hand mirror. I could pass for white again. I repacked my duffel, put my shirt and coat back on and wondered how I could best leave the colored rest room without attracting attention. I guessed it was near midnight, but the traffic in and out remained heavy.

Oddly, there was little of the easy conversation one generally hears in public rest rooms, none of the laughter and "woofing." I waited, listening to footsteps come and go, to the water-sounds of hand-washing and flushing.

Much later, when I heard no more footsteps, I stepped from my cubicle and walked toward the door that led into the main waiting room. I hurried into the crowd unnoticed.

The shift back to white status was always confusing. I had to guard against the easy, semiobscene language that Negroes use among themselves, for coming from a white man it is insulting. It was midnight. I asked a doorman where to find a room for the night. He indicated a neon sign that stood out against the night sky—YMCA, only a block or so away. I realized that though I was well dressed for a Negro, my appearance looked shabby for a white man. He judged me by that and indicated a place where lodging was inexpensive.

▼ ▼ ▼

DECEMBER 2

Telephone calls to the *Sepia* office in Fort Worth. They asked me to do some more stories about Atlanta. My photographer, Don Rutledge, could not get there for two days. I telephoned the Trappist monastery at Conyers, Georgia, about thirty miles away and asked if they would receive me for a short visit. I felt the past weeks, the strange sickness that cried for a change, for some relief from the constant racial grind.

I checked out of the Y and boarded the bus for Conyers. The driver had mastered one of the techniques of degrading the Negro. Every time a white person got off, the driver said politely: "Watch your step, please." But whenever a Negro approached the front to get off, the driver's silence fairly roared. His refusal to extend even this courtesy to passengers who had paid as much as any white for their tickets was so conspicuous it made me aware of the stirrings of resentment among the Negroes behind me.

Nicely dressed, respectable Negro women, even the aged, could not draw from him the courteous warning, "Watch your step." The implication was eloquently clear and unmistakable.

I watched, wondering at the uselessness of the man's bad manners. Then at a stop, a group of whites walked to the front and behind them a sedately dressed Negro woman in her fifties. I felt the driver's dilemma and was amused by it. Should he say "Watch your step, please," when the statement would be addressed also to the Negro?

"Watch your step, please," he finally said, opening the doors. The whites stepped down without response, but the Negro lady nodded politely to him and said, "Thank you," knowing full well his warning had not been meant for her. It was a moment of triumph. She proved herself more courteous than his white passengers and more courteous than he; and she did it without the slightest sarcasm. The subtlety of it escaped the whites on the bus, but it in no way escaped the driver or the Negroes at the back. I heard stifled chuckles of approval from behind me. The driver slammed the doors harder than necessary and lurched the bus forward.

I arrived at the Trappist monastery with its two thousand acres of woods and farmlands and entered the courtyard as the monks were chanting Vespers. Their voices floated to me. A brown-robed Brother led me to a cell on the second floor and informed me supper would be at five.

The contrast was almost too great to be borne. It was a shock, like walking from the dismal swamps into sudden brilliant sunlight. Here all was peace, all silence except for the chanted prayers. Here men know nothing of hatred. They sought to make themselves conform ever more perfectly to God's will, whereas outside I had seen mostly men who sought to make God's will conform to their wretched prejudices. Here men sought their center in God, whereas outside they sought it in themselves. The difference was transforming.

We had supper at five—homemade bread, butter, milk, red beans, spinach and a peach.

At six thirty we went into the chapel for the last prayers of the day. I knelt in the chapel balcony, looking down on ninety white-robed monks. When Compline was finished, they turned out most of the lights and chanted the solemn *Salve Regina* so beautifully, so tenderly, we felt the crusts of our lives fall away and we rested in the deep hush of eternity. When the last echoes died to silence the monks filed out. Another day had ended for them. They went to bed at seven and would get up to begin a new day in the morning at two. The same thing has happened in Trappist monasteries throughout the centuries. I felt the timelessness of it and I remained a long time alone in the darkened chapel—not praying, simply resting in the warmth where all senses are ordered into harmony, where hatred cannot penetrate. After my weeks of travel, when I had seen constantly the rawness of man's contempt for man, the mere act of resting in this atmosphere was healing.

I went down the hall to take a shower and wash my clothes in the sink. As I returned to my cell, I found a monk, the guestmaster, who had come to see if I needed anything. We talked for a time and I explained my research project to him.

"Do Negroes often come here as guests, to spend a few days, Father?" I asked.

"Oh yes," he said. "Though I don't suppose many really know about this place."

"This is the Deep South," I said. "When you have Negro guests, do you have any trouble with your white guests?"

"No . . . no . . . the type of white man who would come to the Trappists—well, he comes here to be in an atmosphere of dedication to God. Such a man would hardly keep one eye on God and the other on the color of his neighbor's skin."

We discussed the religiosity of the racists. I told him how often I had heard them invoke God, and then some passage from the Bible, and urge all who might be faltering in their racial prejudice to "Pray, brother, with all your heart before you decide to let them niggers into our schools and cafés."

The monk laughed. "Didn't Shakespeare say something about 'every fool in error can find a passage of Scripture to back him up'? He knew his religious bigots."

I showed the priest the booklet on racial justice, *For Men of Good Will,* written by a New Orleans priest, Robert Guste, in which most of the questions and clichés about the Negro are discounted, particularly that God made the Negro dark as a curse. Father Guste says, "No modern Biblical scholar would subscribe to any such theory."

The monk nodded. I insisted on the point. "Is there any-place in the Bible that justifies it—even by a stretch of the imagination, Father?"

"Biblical scholars don't stretch their imaginations—at least reputable ones don't," he said. "Will you wait a moment. I have something you must read."

He returned almost immediately with the book *Scholasticism and Politics,* by Jacques Maritain.

"Maritain has some profound things to say about the religion of racists," he said, leafing the book. "You might review this page." He placed a cardboard marker at the page and handed the book to me.

The monk bowed and left. I listened to the rustle of his thick robes as he walked down the hall in the tremendous silence. I then had a visit from a young college instructor of English—a born Southerner of great breadth of understanding. He told me that his more liberated views of the Negro were in such contradiction to those of his elders, his parents and uncles, that he no longer went home to visit them. We talked until midnight. He invited me to go with him to visit Flannery O'Connor the next day, but I told him that since I had only a few hours, I felt I must spend them in the monastery.

He left. The cell was cold. The Georgia countryside slept outside. Since I would be getting up at two to begin the day, I decided not to sleep. I felt the steam radiator with my hand. It was without a hint of warmth. The Maritain lay on the cot. I got into bed and opened the page the monk had marked.

Speaking of the religiosity of racists, Maritain observes:

God is invoked . . . and He is invoked against the God of the spirit, of intelligence and love—excluding and hating this God. What an extraordinary spiritual phenomenon this is: people believe in God and yet do not know God. The idea of God is affirmed and at the same time disfigured and perverted.

He goes on to say that this kind of religion, which declines wisdom, even though it may call itself Christian, is in reality as anti-Christian as is atheism.

I was startled that the French philosopher could so perfectly characterize the racists of our Southern states. Then I realized that he was describing racists everywhere and from all times—that this is the religious trait of men who twist their minds to consider racial prejudice a virtue—whether it be a White Citizens Council or Klan member, a Nazi *gauleiter*, a South African white supremacist or merely someone's aunt who says, "Nobody's worse than those Italians (or Spaniards, or Englishmen, or Danes, etc.)."

I slept and woke up shouting from the old familiar nightmare of men and women closing in on me, shuffling toward me. I lay there fully dressed under the cell's bare globe, trembling. I felt myself flush with embarrassment at having disturbed the Trappist silence. Surely monks sleeping in other cells, their bodies exhausted from work in the fields and hours of prayers, heard me and lay awake wondering.

▼ ▼ ▼

DECEMBER 4

This morning the young professor drove me back to Atlanta. Along the roadside, oaks were spectacularly red against the green of pines. In town I registered at the

Georgia Hotel, a luxury hotel, where I was treated with the utmost suspicion and discourtesy. Did the staff have doubts about my "racial purity"? Though I had bags and was well enough dressed, they made me pay in advance and I could not make a phone call without their insisting I come down immediately to the desk and pay the dime. I had never encountered such obtuseness in a first-class hotel, and I told them so, but this only increased their inhospitality. I decided not to stay.

The Black Star photographer, Don Rutledge, arrived in his little Renault from Rockvale, Tennessee, around noon. We were to do a story together on Atlanta's Negro business and civic leaders, and perhaps some others. I liked him immediately. He is a tall, somewhat skinny young fellow, married and has a child—a gentleman in every way.

▼ ▼ ▼

DECEMBER 7

Three days of hard work, from morning until late at night. My interview notebooks were filled up, but at night I was too tired to write in my journal and went immediately to bed. We had had the most splendid help and co-operation from such Negro leaders as Attorney A. T. Walden, businessman T. M. Alexander, the Reverend Samuel Williams, and the immensely impressive Dr. Benjamin Mays, president of Morehouse . . . also many others.

I had arrived in Atlanta feeling that the situation for the Negro in the South was utterly hopeless—due to the racists' powerful hold on the purse strings of whites and Negroes alike; and due to the lack of unanimity among Negroes.

But Atlanta changed my mind. Atlanta has gone far in proving that "the Problem" can be solved and in showing us the way to do it. Though segregation and discrimination still prevail and still work a hardship, great strides have been made—strides that must give hope to every observer of the South.

At least three factors are responsible:

First and most important, the Negroes have united in a common goal and purpose; and Atlanta has more men of leadership quality than any other city in the South—men of high education, long vision and great dynamism.

Second, as one of the leaders, Mr. T. M. Alexander, explained to me, though the State of Georgia has never had an administration sympathetic to the Negro cause, the city of Atlanta has long been favored with an enlightened administration, under the leadership of Mayor William B. Hartsfield.

Third, the city has been blessed by a newspaper, the *Atlanta Constitution*, that is not afraid to take a stand for right and justice. Its most noted columnist (and now publisher), Ralph McGill, Pulitzer Prize winner, is significantly referred to as "Rastus" by the White Citizens Councils.

In the South, where most newspapers, even the great metropolitan dailies, have shown themselves shortsighted and uncourageous or—worse—have propagandized as though they were organs of the Councils and Klans, the importance of those newspapers that live up to their journalistic responsibilities cannot be sufficiently emphasized. A handful of the latter, headed by such men as Mark Ethridge, Hodding Carter, Easton King, Harry Golden, P. D. East and Ralph McGill, plus a few others, have stood up for the freedoms of all men.

McGill and his colleagues gamble their fortunes and their reputations on the proposition that it is journalism's sacred trust to find and publish the truth and that the majority, if properly informed, will act for the good of the community and the country. The great danger in the South comes precisely from the fact that the public is not informed. Newspapers shirk notoriously their editorial responsibilities and print what they think their readers want. They lean with the prevailing winds and employ every fallacy of logic in order to editorialize harmoniously with popular prejudices. They also keep a close eye on possible economic reprisals from the Councils and the Klans, plus other superpatriotic groups who bring pressures to bear

on the newspapers' advertisers. In addition, most adhere
to the long-standing conspiracy of silence about anything
remotely favorable to the Negro. His achievements are
carefully excluded or, when they demand attention, they
are handled with the greatest care to avoid the impression
that anything good the individual Negro does is typical
of his race.

We spent our time, significantly, between the three-
block section on Auburn Street where Negro financing and
industry controls some eighty million dollars, and the section of the six Negro colleges. A close parallel exists
between the two, for most of the business leaders are connected with the schools of higher learning, either as teachers or directors. In addition, all of these men are religious
leaders in the community. As Alexander stated: "If we
know anything, it is that if virtues do not equal powers,
the powers will be misused."

About twenty-five years ago two men came to Atlanta
to teach in the university system. Both were economists.
They found Atlanta a thriving intellectual center for the
Negro. In the slave years any attempt at literacy among
Negroes was severely punished. In some communities a
Negro's right hand was mutilated if he learned to read and
write. The Negro therefore prized education as the only
doorway into the world of knowledge and dignity to which
he aspired. The climate was right to begin a program that
would lead them to economic respectability. L. D. Milton
and J. B. Blayton, the two economists, recognized that so
long as the Negro had to depend on white banks to finance
his projects for improvement and growth, he was at the
mercy of the white man. They recognized that economic
emancipation was the key to the racial solution. So long as
the race had to depend on a basically hostile source of
financing, it would not advance, since the source would
simply refuse loans for any project that did not meet with
its approval.

These two men said in essence: "Let everyone in the
community pool what little resources he has with others."
By uniting the small power of small sums, by skillfully
manipulating it, they could achieve a consolidated financial
power. This action resulted in the founding of two banks in

Atlanta. Recently, I discovered, an instance arose where the Negro leaders used their economic leverage in a typical manner. It became necessary for the Negro community to expand its physical limits. An area of white residences served as a bottleneck. The housing committee met and Negroes and whites alike agreed to have Negroes purchase this block of homes. The white lending agencies, however, refused to make the loans. As usual the Negro leaders called a meeting to discuss what might be done. They agreed to set aside a large sum of money from which applicants could make loans to buy these houses. After four such loans were made, the white lending agencies called and said: "Don't take all that business away from us. How about letting us handle a few of those loans?" Business that had been refused a few days previously was now welcomed.

But though financing is the key, other elements are no less important. Education, housing, job opportunities and the vote enter the picture of any improving community. The Negro leader, the "successful" man in Atlanta, is deeply imbued with a sense of responsibility toward his community. This is true of the doctors, the lawyers, the educators, the religious leaders and the businessmen.

"There is no 'big Me' and 'little you,'" T. M. Alexander, one of the founders of the Southeastern Fidelity Fire Insurance Company, said. "We must pool all of our resources, material and mental, to gain the respect that will enable all of us to walk the streets with the dignity of American citizens."

In the matter of education, Atlanta has long been eminent. With men of the quality of Benjamin Mays, president of Morehouse, and Rufus Clement, president of Atlanta University—to mention only two who are world-renowned —the intellectual climate is of high quality. The most impressive proof of this is found in the classrooms where teachers and students face squarely the problems that haunt this country, particularly the race problem. I visited the sociology class of Spelman College where Dr. Moreland (Mrs. Charles Moreland), bullied and taunted and challenged her class to think and talk. This handsome and brilliant young woman, like her students, despises the idea that in America any man has to "earn" his rights to first-class citizenship. But she and her colleagues believe, on the other hand, that every citizen has to live up to his duties of citizenship. In the classes I attended, one of the students was assigned to take the role of the white racist, and to argue his points to the other students. It was a brutal and revealing session. The comparison between them and the white racists was cruel indeed. The students have better manners, more learning, more courtesy and infinitely more understanding.

Every leader is interested in better housing. Many professional men, particularly doctors like F. Earl McLendon, have developed residential areas as their contribution to the cause. Atlanta has virtually miles and miles of splendid Negro homes. They have destroyed the cliché that whenever Negroes move into an area the property values go down. In every instance, they have improved the homes they have bought from the whites and built even better ones. The philosophy here is simple. Try to anchor as many Negroes as possible in their own homes.

The fourth element, the vote, the right of the governed to govern themselves, has long been a cherished goal of all thinking men of Atlanta. Every business, professional and civic leader is also a leader in politics. In 1949, the Democrats, under A. T. Walden, and the Republicans, under John Wesley Dobbs, united to form the Atlanta Negro Voters League; and the Negro began to have a voice in his government. It has become an increasingly important and responsible one. By 1955 this type of political action helped elect Atlanta University President Rufus E. Clement to the city school board, making him the first Negro to hold elective office in George since the Reconstruction.[1]

All take into account the cooperation of a fair-minded city administration under the leadership of Mayor Hartsfield. Almost alone among politicians of the South, Mayor Hartsfield has not sunk to the level of winning votes at the Negro's expense. He has proved the point that a man can, after all, stand up for justice and constitutional law and still not sacrifice his political career.

[1] Bardolph, *The Negro Vanguard*, New York: Rinehart & Co., 1959.

Benjamin Mays, J. B. Blayton, L. D. Milton, A. T. Walden, John Wesley Dobbs, Norris Herndon of the Atlantic Life Insurance Company, banker-druggist C. R. Yates, W. J. Shaw, E. M. Martin, Rev. Samuel Williams, Rev. William Holmes Borders, Rev. H. I. Bearden, Rev. Martin Luther King, Sr., and his son, Martin Luther King, Jr.— each has contributed and continues to contribute to the American dream in its best sense.

I recall scenes picked at random:

The look of growing concern and perhaps humiliation on photographer Don Rutledge's face as we moved from one scene to another—concern and humiliation to realize that these men, these scenes, these ideals were unknown to most Americans and utterly beyond the comprehension of the Southern racist. It was a look, however, overspread with delight;

The look of surprise and vast amusement on Dr. Benjamin Mays's intelligent face when I confided to him my journey as a Negro;

At Spelman College, hearing Rosalyn Pope play magnificently the Bach Toccata in D, and then the strange, bewildered expression on her face when she told me about arriving in Paris to spend a year studying piano—the strangeness of living in a great city where she could attend concerts to her fill, where she could walk into any door, where she was a human being first and last and not dismissed as a "Negro";

The evening in T. M. Alexander's home, the talk with his wife and his brilliant children: "We realize that we have to run just to keep up." They are intent, like the other members of the community, upon doing everything within their power to nullify the picture of the loud, the brassy, the pushy and "successful" Negro;

Long talk with the Reverend Samuel Williams in his living room. A forceful man, but quiet, of fine intellect. Professor of Philosophy. "I spent years," he told me, "studying the phenomenon of love."

"And I spend years studying the phenomenon of justice."

"At base, we spend years studying the same thing."

It was time to return to New Orleans. My assignments

in Atlanta with Rutledge were finished. He was anxious to get back to his wife and child. I asked him if he knew a first-rate photographer in New Orleans, since I wanted to go back over the terrain again as a Negro and have photos made. The project fascinated him and we arranged to drive to New Orleans together so he could photograph it.

▼ ▼ ▼

DECEMBER 9

In New Orleans I resumed my Negro identity and we went to all of my former haunts to photograph them.

Getting photos proved a problem. A Negro being photographed by a white arouses suspicions. Whites tended to wonder, "What Negro celebrity is he?" and to presume I was uppity. It equally aroused the curiosity of the Negroes. The "Uncle Toms" think that every Negro should bury his head in the sand and pretend he is not there. They distrust any Negro prominent enough to be photographed by a white photographer. Others feared I might be an Uncle Tom going over to the white side.

We had to arrange to be at the same spot at the same time, but pretended to have no relationship. Rutledge appeared to be simply another tourist taking photos, and I just happened to be in them.

One day we got some unexpected help. He approached a fruit stand in the French market and began making photographs. I walked up from another direction and bought some walnuts and an apple. An elderly and civil woman waited on me while another woman talked to him some distance away. She said, "Why don't you hurry up and get a picture of that funny old nigger before he leaves?" Rutledge said he believed he would, and I, pretending to be unaware of the plot, obliged by hanging around the fruit stalls.

An hour later we went into the fish market. I showed

interest in buying a fish and at that moment Rutledge walked up and asked the vendor if he minded being photographed with some of the fish. The vendor was delighted. He left me standing at the counter and went to pose with a giant fish in his hand. I followed, pretending to think this was the fish he would sell me. Trying not to be impolite to me, he nevertheless maneuvered every possible way to keep me out of the pictures, and finally, when I stuck close to him, he became irritated and told me customers weren't allowed behind the counter. Then, when Rutledge said: "That's good right there, hold it," the man faced front and gave his most winning smile. A nod from Rutledge told me we had enough pictures, so I drifted away and out the door.

We returned to the shoe stand, where we had no problem since my old partner, Sterling Williams, was intelligent and knowledgeable. Otherwise we had to take the pictures quickly and disappear before a crowd gathered and began to ask questions.

The experience had subtler points that did not escape Rutledge. Having a Negro for a companion took him inside the problem. He could avail himself of any rest room, any water fountain, any café for a cup of coffee; but he could not take me with him. Needless to say, he was too much of a gentleman to do this, and there were times when we went without that cup of coffee or that glass of water.

▼　▼　▼

DECEMBER 14

Finally the photos were taken, the project concluded, and I resumed for the final time my white identity. I felt strangely sad to leave the world of the Negro after having shared it so long—almost as though I were fleeing my share of his pain and heartache.

▼　▼　▼

DECEMBER 15, MANSFIELD, TEXAS

I sat in the jet this afternoon, flying home from New Orleans, and looked out the window to the patterns of a December countryside far below. And I felt the greatest love for this land and the deepest dread of the task that now lay before me—the task of telling truths that would make me and my family the target of all the hate groups.

But for the moment, the joyful expectation of seeing my wife and children again after seven weeks overwhelmed all other feelings.

When the plane landed, I hurried to collect my bags and walk out front. The car soon arrived, with children waving and shouting from the windows. I felt their arms around my neck, their hugs and the marvelous jubilation of reunion. And in the midst of it, the picture of the prejudice and bigotry from which I had just come flashed into my mind, and I heard myself mutter: "My God, how can men do it when there are things like this in the world?"

The faces of my wife and mother spoke their relief that it was over.

That night was a festival. The country was aromatic with late autumn, with the love of family, with the return to light and affection. We talked little about the experience. It was too near, too sore. We talked with the children, about the cats and the farm animals.

▼ ▼ ▼

JANUARY 2

Mr. Levitan, the owner of *Sepia*, called and asked me to come in for an editorial conference with Mrs. Jackson.

Though the magazine had paid for the trip, and I in turn promised them some articles about it, he gave me the opportunity to back out. "It'll cause trouble," he said. "We don't want to see you killed. What do you think? Hadn't we better forget the whole thing?"

"Do you mean you're willing to cancel this, after all you've been led to expect?" I asked.

"The only way I'll run it is if you insist," he said.

"Then I think we must run it," I said, wishing with all my heart I could drop it. However, *Sepia*, unlike many magazines, is widely read in the Deep South by Negroes. I felt it was the best way of letting them know that their condition was known, that the world knew more about them than they suspected; the best way to give them hope.

The world would know, then, in early March. It was January. I had two months left in which to work before the storm would break.

▼ ▼ ▼

FEBRUARY 26

The time drew to a close. The news became known. I had spent weeks at work, studying, correlating statistics, going through reports, none of which actually help to reveal the truth of what it is like to be discriminated against. They cancel truth almost more than they reveal it. I decided to throw them away and simply publish what happened to me.

A call from Hollywood. Paul Coates spoke to me, asked me to fly out and be on his interview program. I accepted.

▼ ▼ ▼

MARCH 14

The first of the Coates shows was televised locally after it had been given heavy publicity over the weekend by the newspapers. I think almost every TV viewer in the area watched the show.

When the program was finished, and we heard Paul Coates announce we would return "tomorrow" to continue the interview, our attention switched to the telephone. We realized that now our neighbors knew, now the whole Dallas-Fort Worth area knew.

The phone began to ring. I picked it up, wondering what I should say if it were an abusive call. It was Penn and L. A. Jones from Midlothian. They talked for a long time. I realized that they were tying up the line so that no hate calls could come through. Finally, after almost an hour, we said good-by. Immediately my parents called to say it was fine. How full of dread their voices were—but they sincerely approved of what I had said.

After that, silence. We sat and waited, but the phone did not ring. The silence was so unnatural, so ominous, it weighed heavy on us. Were none of my friends, no other members of my family going to call?

▼ ▼ ▼

MARCH 17

Flew to New York two days ago. Interview this morning with *Time* magazine in their new offices. They took photos and treated me with great cordiality. While I was at *Time*, the Dave Garroway show called. We were to have a preliminary interview that afternoon at five.

Unable to bear the silence from home, I returned to my room and telephoned to Mansfield. As a result of the two Paul Coates shows, my mother had received her first threatening call. It was from a woman who would not identify herself. The conversation had begun politely enough. The woman said they could not understand in town how I could turn against my own race. My mother assured her I had done this precisely *for* my race. The woman said: "Why he's just thrown the door wide open for those niggers, and after we've *all* worked so hard to keep them out." She then became abusive and succeeded in terrorizing my mother by telling her, "If you could just hear what they're planning to do to him if he ever comes back to Mansfield—"

"Who's planning?" my mother asked.

"That's all right. You just ought to be over at Curry's [a local café and night spot on the highway leading into Mansfield, run by ardent segregationists]. You'd see to it he never showed his face in Mansfield again."

My mother said she felt better when I talked to her. She had never been confronted with this sort of brutality before. She called my wife over and they sat together, frightened. Then they called Penn Jones, who came immediately and placed himself at their disposition.

Sickened that they would pick on a man's mother and strike at him through terrorizing her, I immediately made calls and asked for police surveillance of both my home and my parents' home.

▼ ▼ ▼

MARCH 18

Garroway was immensely impressive. When we finally met this morning, briefly, before I went on camera, I told him I was afraid that my appearance would bring severe repercussions against him from the South. He stood large, much larger than he appears on the screen. I told him I would answer his questions as carefully as posible. He bent over me and said: "Mr. Griffin—John—let me just ask you to do one thing."

I braced myself against his request, fearing he would ask me to soft-pedal.

"Just tell the truth as honestly and as frankly as you can and don't worry about my sponsors or anything else. You keep your mind clear to answer whatever I ask. Will you forget everything else and just remember that?"

I looked at him with a resurgence of faith in a public figure. He kept me on camera twenty minutes and he asked pointed questions that did not evade the issue. Before the interview was over, we were both deeply moved. At the end he asked me about discrimination in the North. I told him I was not competent to answer. I told him that the Southern racist invariably brought up the point that things aren't perfect in the North either—which is no doubt so—as though that fact justified his injustices in the South.

▼ ▼ ▼

MARCH 23

It was a busy weekend. I spent more and more time in my room between interviews and conferences with Mr. Levitan and our PR man, Benn Hall, while Mr. Levitan had a constant stream of visitors in his suite.

On Tuesday I did a TV documentary with Harry Golden. The Mike Wallace show went on that evening, and then a long radio interview on the Long John show from midnight until four thirty in the morning. I got no sleep. Benn Hall offered me tranquilizers, but I did not dare take one for fear it would put me out completely. The *Time* article would be out that evening. I was anxious to see how they

would treat the story. But I was most nervous about the
Mike Wallace show, and told Benn Hall that if Wallace
asked just one wrong question, I would get up and walk
out. He assured me Wallace would be sympathetic, but I
had strong reservations. I particularly feared he would get
embroiled in a religious discussion, bring in my Roman
Catholicism in a way that could embarrass the Church.

The Golden show went all right. It was easy, with the
director taking pains to keep it informal and to encourage
me. I got off to a bad start, but we did it over and it came
out all right.

Then, in the evening, Benn Hall came to pick me up.
We took a taxi to Mike Wallace's office, stopping at the
corner of Broadway and 14th to pick up a copy of *Time*.
It was around eight o'clock and the streets were wet under
a drizzling rain. Benn left me in a cigar stand and ran
across the street to get the magazine. In a moment he
returned with two copies. The story was good—they had
told it right and straight. Relieved, we walked to Wallace's
office.

When they showed us in, Wallace rose from his chair
behind the desk and shook hands. I was surprised to find
him so much more youthful in appearance than I had
imagined; but he looked also tired and uncomfortable. He
offered me a seat and without pretense asked if I wanted
to see the questions he planned to ask me. I told him no.
He appeared to know that I viewed him cautiously and
that I was not enthusiastic about this interview. He fumbled
uncomfortably for words and I took a liking to him. From
the hints he dropped ("We've investigated you pretty
thoroughly"), I was aghast—he knew things about the
trip, the names of people I had stayed with—many things
I had tried to hide in order to protect the people involved.

"Please," I pleaded. "Don't mention those names on the
air. I'd be afraid their lives would be endangered, and
they were my friends."

"Hell—I'm not going to do a damned thing to hurt
them," he said. "Look—I'm on your side."

"How did you find out about all of this?" I asked.

"Oh, it's part of the business," he said.

We sat in his office, both of us dull, both of us tired to death. Our talk frittered out. He asked how the Coates shows went, said he heard they were excellent. "That makes me want to do better," he said.

"He had a full hour—you've only got a half hour," I said.

He pulled a bottle of whisky out of his desk, offered me a drink. I refused. "Look, John—hell, I know you've done nothing but answer questions on all these shows and newspaper interviews; but will you pull yourself together and really work for me tonight?"

"I'd do that as a matter of conscience anyway," I said.

"You want me to tell you something," he said. "I'm scared to death of you—I mean a man who'd do what you've done—"

"Then you don't know me as well as I thought you did," I said. "The truth is I'm scared to death of you."

He burst out laughing. "Well, I guarantee you, you've got no reason to be."

Liveliness returned. Both of us felt certain it would go well.

We walked out onto a stage that contained only two chairs and a smoking stand. The camera technicians and director prepared us, got cables out of sight, strapped mikes on our necks, shouted instructions. Wallace smoked incessantly and smiled at me while yelling oaths in answer to yelled instructions. "Remember," he said. "We've got to do as well in a half hour as you did with Paul in an hour."

"I'll talk fast," I said, peering past the lights into the camera jumble of darkness.

The count started. The red lights came on. Wallace talked and smoked. He poured intelligent questions into me and kept his face close, absorbing my attention, encouraging me. It was a supercharged moment. I answered, forgetting everything except him and his questions. Fatigue disappeared. Fascination took over. The excitement sustained us. I realized, when the time was up, that it had gone well. And when we went off the air, Wallace shouted, "Top notch. Cancel everything and schedule it immediately."

It was an extraordinary experience. Never have I been handled more superbly by an interviewer.

▼ ▼ ▼

APRIL 1

Radio-Television Française flew a crew of five from Paris to do a television show of the person-to-person type at my home in Mansfield. We had three busy days, with Pierre Dumayet, the commentator, and Claude Loursaid, the director of the *Cinq Colonnes à la Une*. I put them on the plane out of here yesterday evening, and only then had time to settle down to some work. But work was difficult. The story had circulated all over the world, and mail, telegrams and telephone calls poured in.

The local situation was odd. I had no contact with any- one in town and no one had contact with me. However, I understood that I was loudly discussed in the stores and on the streets—that the druggist and a couple of others had risen to my defense when the discussions became hot. I avoided going downtown, going into any of the stores for fear my presence would embarrass people who had been my friends.

The local roadside café, a gathering place for the segre- gationists, had a new sign. For some time it had carried a sign reading WE DON'T SERVE NEGROES. Then this was replaced by a larger sign: WHITES ONLY. Now another had joined it: NO ALBINOS ALLOWED. This sign that so disgusted my parents greatly amused me. I was surprised and pleased to discover that Foy Curry, the café-owner, was, after all, a man of some wit.

The principal point of contention among the women of the town appeared to be whether or not I had done a "Christian" thing. I feel that though few of them liked it, at least a large proportion of them understood that I worked as much for them and their children as I did for the Negroes. Certainly, my mail thus far was overwhelmingly congratulatory. I began to hope that I had been overly pessimistic, that we might be able to live in Mansfield in an atmosphere of peace and understanding after all.

▼ ▼ ▼

APRIL 2

The phone woke me in the morning. I glanced out our front window to a calm spring landscape of fields and woods, then picked up the phone. A long-distance call from the *Star-Telegram* in Fort Worth. What could they want? I wondered, since they had not carried one word about my story. The reporter came on the line. He cautiously asked me how things were.

"All right as far as I know," I said.

"You don't sound too excited," he said. I began to feel uneasy.

"Why should I be?"

"You mean you haven't heard?"

"What?"

"You were hanged in effigy from the center red-light wire downtown on Main Street this morning."

"In Mansfield?" I asked.

"That's right." He told me that the *Star-Telegram* had received an anonymous call that racists had hanged my effigy on Main Street. The newspaper checked it out with the local constable who confirmed that a dummy, half black, half white, with my name on it and a yellow streak painted down its back, was hanging from the wire.

"What would you like to say about it?" the reporter asked.

"I'm sorry it happened," I said. "It'll only give the town a worse name."

"People seem pretty excited about what you've done.

There's a lot of loose talk out in Mansfield. Do you think this represents a real threat?"

"I'd probably be the last to know," I said.

"Do you think your life's in danger?"

"I have no idea."

"What are you going to do about this hanging?"

"Ignore it."

"You're not even going downtown to see it?"

"No . . . this sort of thing is not interesting," I said.

"Do you think this represents the prevailing sentiment around town?"

"No, I'm sure it doesn't."

The reporter thanked me for my answers. He said they had sent a photographer out to take a picture of the effigy.

The reporter called back. He wondered, as I did, how this could have happened on Main Street when we are supposed to have police on duty all night. He told me that a grocer saw the effigy around 5 A.M. when he came to work, called the constable and told him to "get that damned thing down from there." The constable had taken it down and thrown it onto the town junk heap, but when the reporter and photographer got to Mansfield, someone had retrieved the effigy from the dump and hung it on a sign reading: $25.00 FINE FOR DUMPING DEAD ANIMALS.

The local people remained utterly silent. I waited for just one, anyone, to call and say: "We may not approve of your views, but we think this hanging is shameful." Their silence was eloquent and devastating. My disappointment grew as the afternoon passed. Did their silence condone the lynching? My family's uneasiness approached terror now. My parents and my wife's mother begged us to take the children and go away somewhere until this thing blew over.

That evening the *Star-Telegram* carried a six-column banner front-page headline announcing the lynching in effigy. Margaret Ann Turner (Mrs. Decherd Turner) had heard the news on TV and called from Dallas to say they were coming after the children. We telephoned the Joneses at Midlothian and then called the Turners back. Decherd said we must come and stay with them as long as there was the slightest danger. The Joneses also invited us, but they felt it might be better if we were in Dallas, since I had much support there, according to them.

At such times, the slightest kindness on the part of anyone becomes a sort of bravery. My dad who had gone to town, defiantly I imagine, returned almost jubilant. He had gone into the grocery store where he usually trades and heard the sudden silence. Then one of the owners, in the back at the meat counter, called a greeting.

"I didn't know whether I was still welcome," Dad said.

"Hell, you know better than that," the grocer shouted.

"I don't know—the way people have been acting. I was afraid if they saw me coming into your store, they might stop trading here."

"That's the kind of customer we don't want in the first place," the grocer said.

In the context of the day, this was heroism. Someone in town dared to express an opinion.

The time came to take my wife and children to Dallas. Decherd Turner had called again and told me to bring my typewriter and current work. "We've fixed you up an office here at the Bridwell Library," he said, referring to the library of the Southern Methodist University Perkins School of Theology.

"I'm not going to do it. Somebody's sure to find out and they'll make a squawk about H.M.U. offering me protection. I'm too unpopular. I don't want to get you or them into any uncomfortable situation."

He insisted. He said they would be honored to offer me any hospitality and library or research facilities. They even requested I lecture to the student body.

On my way out of the lane that leads from my parents' place to my home, the neighbors at the halfway point waved, but those near the highway—people with whom we have been cordial—gave me the most violently hostile stare. I ran the gantlet driving through town. At the second red light a truck pulled up beside me and a young man in a cowboy hat looked down into the cab of my car. He told me he'd heard talk that "they" were planning to come and castrate me, that the date had been set. He said this coldly, without emotion, neither threatening nor sympathetic, exactly the way one would say: "The weatherman's promising rain for tomorrow." I stared up at him, not recognizing him, and felt my face flush with the embarrassment of being a public spectacle. After he drove on, I felt sure he meant to imply that someone from out of town, not a local group, planned this.

When I got home, the suitcases were packed. My wife's mother said people in town thought the effigy-hanging was the work of "outsiders." I told her I had no way of knowing but would certainly like to believe it.

▼ ▼ ▼

APRIL 7

The *Star-Telegram* carried an excellent and accurate story as a follow-up to the effigy hanging. It made things clear, it clarified motives and it certainly lifted the entire matter above segregation and desegregation.

Yet we learned that they burned a cross just above our house at the Negro school, and that someone remarked they should have burned it on my land. I wish they had, I wish they had—it would have been far better than burning it at the school.

The Turners crowded us into their house. The relief to be there, surrounded by friends, away from the hostility and the threats of the bullies and castraters, was so great that we were suddenly filled with exhaustion.

▼ ▼ ▼

APRIL 11

We returned to Mansfield, deciding to hide away no longer. The mail poured in, hearteningly favorable and moving. Most people in other areas, including the Deep South, understood, though the situation remained uncomfortable at home. Our townspeople wanted to "keep things peaceful" at all costs. They said I had "stirred things up." This is laudable and tragic. I, too, say let us be peaceful; but the only way to do this is first to assure justice. By keeping "peaceful" in this instance, we end up consenting to the destruction of all peace—for so long as we condone injustice by a small but powerful group, we condone the destruction of all social stability, all real peace, all trust in man's good intentions toward his fellow man.

▼ ▼ ▼

JUNE 19, FATHER'S DAY

There were six thousand letters to date and only nine of them abusive. Many favorable letters came from Deep South states, from the whites. This confirmed my contention that the average Southern white is more properly disposed than he dares allow his neighbor to see, that he is more afraid of his fellow white racist than he is of the Negro.

Justice Bok sent me a copy of his controversial speech at Radcliffe. He put it clearly:

I am an Angry Old Man about racial segregation. I live in a city where twenty-five per cent of the population is Negro and I doubt that the percentage is much higher, except in spots, in the eleven Civil War States. I am angry at being told I cannot understand the problem. I do not believe that it takes a genius to pierce to the heart of a situation to which Southern chivalry once gave, among other things, the mulatto. The cry about lack of understanding and the need for time to work things out are only excuses to do little or nothing about them, and for almost a hundred years this served the South very well. . . . With all of the pious talk against Communism, the present conflict over integration is doing the work of the

Communists almost better than they could do it themselves.
This is to our shame when we should be sharpening and per-
fecting our procedures . . . it is only a mixture of ignorance
and conceit that leads one section of the country to assume
that no human beings on earth but themselves can understand
the conditions under which they live.

I am annoyed by those who love mankind but are cruel
and discourteous to people.[1]

I worked all afternoon and then went home and took a
cold shower. Returning to my office in the evening, the
desolation of a little town on a frightfully hot Sunday struck
me. And it struck me, too, that no one there forgets, no
one there forgives. I ran the lines of disapproval every
time I drove through town to my office at the edge of the
woods. This afternoon the town had been deserted except
for the loafers who stood around the filling station and the
street corners. All of them eyed me with animosity. Teen-
age boys in their jeans lounged against building fronts.
They stared. One of the town's citizens who had been
cordial to me drove up and stopped beside me at the red
light. I waved. He looked grimly away, not wanting the
loungers to see him make a friendly gesture, not wanting
them to carry tales. I smelled the sun-softened asphalt,
smelled the summer odors of clover, swallowed the rebuff
and drove on. But I found myself looking down the country
lane that leads to the barn, checking to make certain no
one's car blocked the path.

The lane was clear, but the neighbors were out in their
yard. The woman stared hard at her feet. The husband
lifted his head from weeding and glared at me as I drove
past. I fixed my gaze on the sandy ruts and looked neither
to right nor left. (I had tried nodding too many times.) In
my rear-view mirror, I saw them after I had passed, saw
them stand there like statues peering after me through the
fog of pink dust raised by my wheels.

[1] Curtis Bok, Justice of the Supreme Court of Pennsylvania, speech
at Radcliffe College Commencement, 1960.

▼   ▼   ▼

AUGUST 14

It was late in the afternoon of a cloudy, humid day. My parents, unable to bear the hostility, had sold their home and all their furniture and left for Mexico where they hoped to find a new life. We, too, were going, since we had decided that it was too great an injustice to our children to remain.

But I felt I must remain a while longer, until the bullies had a chance to carry out their threats against me. I could not allow them to say they had "chased" me out. They had promised to fix me on July 15th, and now they said they would do it August 15th.

Across the pastures, the incredible vulgarity of highly amplified hillbilly music drifted from the café on the highway. I sat in the barren studio where I had worked so many years, emptied now of all except the table and the typewriter and the bed, stripped of its sheets, with only the mattress ticking staring up at the ceiling. Empty bookshelves surrounded me. A few yards away, my parents' house stood equally empty. I wandered back and forth from my barn to the house.

▼ ▼ ▼

AUGUST 17

I stayed on, and the lane leading to my barn office remained empty. They did not come for me.

I hired a Negro youth to come and help me clean up my parents' house so it would be spotless for the new owners.

155

The youth knew me and had no reticence in talking since he was sure I was "one of them" so to speak. Both Negroes and whites have gained this certainty from the experiment —because I was a Negro for six weeks, I remained partly Negro or perhaps essentially Negro.

While we swept and burned old newspapers, we talked.

"Why do the whites hate us—we don't hate them?" he asked.

We had a long conversation during which he brought out the obvious fact that whites teach their children to call them "niggers." He said this happened to him all the time and that he would not even go into white neighborhoods because it sickened him to be called that. He said revealing things:

"Your children don't hate us, do they?"

"God, no," I said. "Children have to be taught that kind of filth. We'd never permit ours to learn it."

"Dr. Cook's like that. His little girl called me nigger and he told her if he ever heard her say that again he'd spank her till she couldn't sit down."

The Negro does not understand the white any more than the white understands the Negro. I was dismayed to see the extent to which this youth exaggerated—how could he do otherwise?—the feelings of the whites toward Negroes. He thought they all hated him.

The most distressing repercussion of this lack of communication has been the rise in racism among Negroes, justified to some extent, but a grave symptom nevertheless. It only widens the gap that men of good will are trying desperately to bridge with understanding and compassion. It only strengthens the white racist's cause. The Negro who turns now, in the moment of near-realization of his liberties, and bares his fangs at a man's whiteness, makes the same tragic error the white racist has made.

And it is happening on a wider scale. Too many of the more militant leaders are preaching Negro superiority. I pray that the Negro will not miss his chance to rise to greatness, to build from the strength gained through his past suffering and, above all, to rise beyond vengeance.

If some spark does set the keg afire, it will be a senseless tragedy of ignorant against ignorant, injustice answering injustice—a holocaust that will drag down the innocent and right-thinking masses of human beings.

Then we will all pay for not having cried for justice long ago.

EPILOGUE

What's Happened Since
Black Like Me

The experiment that led to writing *Black Like Me* was done at the very end of 1959, before the first "freedom rides" or any other manifestation of national concern about racial injustice. It was undertaken to discover if America was involved in the practice of racism against black Americans. Most white Americans denied any taint of racism and really believed that in this land we judged every man by his qualities as a human individual. In those days, any mention of racism brought to the public's mind the Nazi suppression of Jewish people, the concentration camps, the gas chambers—and certainly, we protested, we were not like that.

If we could not accept our somewhat different practice of racist suppression of black Americans, how could we ever hope to correct it? Our experience with the Nazis had shown one thing: where racism is practiced, it damages the whole community, not just the victim group.

Were we racists or were we not? That was the important thing to discover. Black men told me that the only way a white man could hope to understand anything about this reality was to wake up some morning in a black man's skin. I decided to try this in order to test this one thing. In order to make the test, I would alter my pigment and shave my head, but change nothing else about myself. I would keep my clothing, my speech patterns, my credentials, and I would answer every question truthfully.

Therefore, if we did, as we claimed, judge each man by his quality as a human individual, my life as a black John Howard Griffin would not be greatly changed, since I was that same human individual, altered only in appearance.

If, on the other hand, we looked at men, saw the mark of pigment, applied all the false "racial and ethnic characteristics," then since I bore that mark, my life would be changed in ways I could not anticipate.

I learned within a very few hours that no one was judging me by my qualities as a human individual and everyone was judging me by my pigment. As soon as white men or women saw me, they automatically assumed I possessed a whole set of false characteristics (false not only to me but to all black men). They could not see me or any other black man as a human individual because they buried us under the garbage of their stereotyped view of us. They saw us as "different" from themselves in fundamental ways: we were irresponsible; we were different in our sexual morals; we were intellectually limited; we had a God-given sense of rhythm; we were lazy and happy-go-lucky; we loved watermelon and fried chicken. How could white men ever really know black men if on every contact the white man's stereotyped view of the black man got in the way? I never knew a black man who felt this stereotyped view fit him. Always, in every encounter even with "good whites," we had the feeling that the white person was not talking with us but with his image of us.

"But," white men would protest, "they really *are* like that. I've known hundreds of them and they're always the same." White men would claim black men were really happy; they liked it that way.

And in a sense, such white men had good evidence for these claims, because if black men did not, in those days, play the stereotyped role of the "good Negro," if he did not do his yessing and grinning and act out the stereotyped image, then he was immediately considered a "bad Negro," called "uppity, smart-alecky, arrogant," and he could lose his job, be attacked, driven away.

White society had everything sewed up. If you didn't grin and yes, you were in deep trouble. If you did, then you allowed white America to go right on believing in the stereotype.

People like Martin Luther King, they said, were just troublemakers and subversives. Whites told their black employees, and really believed it, that the NAACP and Martin Luther King were the black man's greatest enemies. They were offended by any suggestion of injustice. They claimed that they always treated black people wonderfully well and always would so long as black people "stayed in their place." If you asked them what that "place" was, they could not really say, but every black man knew that place was right in the middle of the stereotype.

Often they would face the black employee with this direct question: "Aren't you happy with your situation? Don't I treat you good?" If the black man had any hopes of remaining employed, he had to plaster that smile all over his face and agree.

Once when I was employed at some menial job I noticed that one of the white middle-aged bosses kept looking at me and getting more and more irritated. I could not imagine what I was doing wrong. Certainly I was sad, and that sadness must have shown, for finally he yelled at me: "What's *eating* you, anyway?"

"Nothing," I said.

"Well, what're you so *sullen* about?" he said.

"Nothing," I repeated.

"Well, if you want to hang on to this job, you better show us some teeth."

And I did my grinning.

In those days, the deepest despair hung over the lives of black people, a sense of utter hopelessness, for it seemed that no one in this country knew—or if they knew, couldn't care less—about this hopeless situation.

Good whites—not the type that is overtly bigoted—urged us to "work, study, lift ourselves up by our bootstraps." They really thought that was the remedy. They did not realize that every time black men thought they had found a loophole in the closed society, a way to accomplish this, that loophole was quickly plugged by the consent of all white society. For example, we did not see WHITE ONLY signs on the doors of libraries (where we could find learning and books), but we knew we had better not try to enter one. We saw no WHITE ONLY signs on the doors of schools or universities, but we knew it was suicidal to try to enter one. Above all, that good advice sounded hollow to us because we knew that when men, even educated men, judged you by your pigment, it didn't matter how much you had worked, studied or lifted yourself up. The Ph.D. had to walk just as far to get food, water or restroom facilities as the illiterate, and he could be turned away with the same base discourtesy.

So the predominant feeling was one of hopelessness and despair.

"That white man is not going to let you have anything," black people said.

With the beginning of the freedom rides, the sit-ins, the display of heroic courage and commitment on the part of many who engaged in these activities, and with the rallying around Martin Luther King's philosophy of nonviolent resistance, that feeling of despair began to change into hope. Someone did know. Someone did care. Even white men showed concern. White people like the Markoe brothers, Father John LaFarge, Lillian Smith and others had long pioneered and suffered the fury of racist resentment. Newsmen like P. D. East and other white southerners showed that the white man who advocated that this country live up to its promises to *all* citizens was no more free than any black man. Any white man who advocated justice in those days could be ruined by his white neighbors. This message did not get across to white America. Men kept thinking they were free and that these "rabble-rousers" were really getting what they deserved. Certainly many who had a sense of justice did not dare show it for fear of reprisals. So no one was free, and yet most lived under the delusion that they were free. Heaped on top of the economic reprisals and the dangers of physical reprisal was perhaps the most damaging reprisal of all—the deliberate character assassination that sprang into play the moment a man suggested that there ought to be equality among citizens, and this in a land where we claim equality as a first principle. How easy it was to destroy a man's good name and reputation by suggesting he was in some way subversive or by calling him a communist. This got so bad that concerned people would come to me and say: "I'd like to speak out, but if I do, my neighbors will call me a communist." It got so bad that Lillian Smith wrote: "It's high time we stopped giving the communists credit for every decent, brave, considerate and courteous act" white men might show in regard to black men.

I think the general public has never understood the

"special" kind of life that civil rights advocates had to lead in those years. Racists showed high ingenuity in developing schemes to destroy a man's reputation as a means of nullifying his work. For example, many civil rights advocates, white and black, traveled and lectured extensively. In the early days, a number of effective men were entrapped in situations that either damaged them personally or ruined their reputations. Those who were with lecture bureaus were particularly vulnerable. Anyone could write the lecture bureau for the travel schedules of its speakers. If a man made a long flight to fulfill a speaking engagement, the chances were at least fair that when he landed at the distant airport he might make use of the restroom. It would be enough to plant one or two men in the restroom and accuse him of some indecency. This happened to a Mississippi white attorney in a case that was given maximum publicity in white newspapers. He had to fly to Los Angeles for an appearance. His travel schedule was known. At the end of this flight, he went to the men's restroom, and when he emerged, he was arrested because two men claimed he had indecently exposed himself. He was tried *in absentia* and found guilty in Mississippi. He was publicly labeled a pervert and his career in civil rights was effectively quashed.

Priests openly involved in civil rights advocacy were menaced with rumors that they were immorally involved with women. An Oklahoma priest told me that one day after Mass, when he had given communion to a lady, she met him at the door of the church, gave him a hate stare, and said, "How's your woman, Father?" Priests are accustomed to being called by people in all kinds of distress. Another priest in the South told me a lady called him in distress because she could not understand a certain passage from scripture and wanted to come right over and discuss it with him. He let her come, but when she made advances, he repudiated her and sent her away, fearing it was a scheme of racists to throw a "woman rap" at him.

When Father John Coffield became a public figure because he went into voluntary exile from his diocese in protest against the racial injustices condoned there, he was accepted into the Chicago archdiocese. We feared that he would be victimized by character assassins, perhaps even entrapped into this kind of "woman rap." I went to Chicago to brief him on the precautions he must take now that he stood as a symbol for civil rights, warning him that he must not be alone with any woman, that he must always be able to account for his time so that no one could say he was at such and such a place at such and such a time. He and his host priests were quite dumbfounded. When I saw that they were not really going to believe that men would go to such lengths to vilify Father Coffield, I called Dick Gregory, who happened to be at his home in Chicago. I told him my situation and said I felt Father Coffield would believe him if he would come over and add his warnings to mine. He came to the rectory and we sat up and talked with the priests until six in the morning. He, of course, knew about Father Coffield. He had heard the same rumors I had heard—that Father might be subjected to character assassination. Dick Gregory had already telephoned Chicago's city officials and told them that if there was any attempt on the part of any racist group to smear Father Coffield, Chicago's black citizens would block every freeway leading into the city and tie up Chicago until Father's name was cleared.

We discussed this problem of character assassination and entrapment with Dr. King and Dick Gregory and Whitney Young and other men active in civil rights. We were advised by a black man in the government to take precautions. We should keep our travel schedules secret. We should avoid using public restrooms unless some reliable person accompanied us, to serve as a witness in the event some plant might accuse us of some immoral act or gesture. We were advised never to get maneuvered into a situation where we were alone with any lady we did not know. In the bad days we were even advised to find some pretext of changing our hotel rooms as soon as we registered. Civil rights workers risked being harassed in their hotel rooms. One minister, shortly after arriving at his hotel, answered a knock on his door and was beaten unconscious by two men wielding baseball bats. In my own case, if I stayed more than three days in any large city, I usually tried to change hotels or else move in with some black family. In one city in Louisiana where I lectured, I could not even stay in the city because all the lodging places had been threatened with bombings if they accepted me as a guest.

This kind of thing continued throughout the early and mid-sixties. We led strange, hidden lives. We were advocating only one thing: that this country rid itself of the racism that prevented some citizens from living as fully functioning men and as a result dehumanized all men. We were advocating only that this country live up to its promises to all citizens. But since racism always hides under a respectable guise—usually the guise of patriotism and religion—a great many people loathed us for knocking holes in these respectable guises. It was clear that we would have to live always under threat. When we would get together—with Dick Gregory, Martin Luther King, Sarah Patton Boyle, P. D. East, or any of the hundreds of more or less public advocates of civil rights—we compared notes and discussed this. One thing was clear: we had to accept the fact that these principles were worth dying for, and that there were plenty of people who were willing to see us disappear. In one year we lost seven friends and colleagues in death, of whom only one died a natural death; the others were killed. Dr. King and Dick Gregory became almost fatalistic in accepting the fact that they were dead men and that it was only a matter of time before that fact became a reality. They and many, many others acted with a bravery and heroism almost incomprehensible to most men. They went into areas of extreme danger. This is possible occasionally, but it is almost impossible to keep it up. The human nervous system will not stand it.

I got a glimpse of it up close one day in Chicago when we learned that a black man had been found murdered in a town called Libertyville, in Mississippi. In those days you could only get an "official version" of such events. No black person would talk to you long distance for fear the operator was listening and would report the call. So the official version said simply that the victim, Mr. Lewis Allen, had been found shot, but since he had not been involved in civil rights, it was apparently just an ordinary killing. We did not believe it, so we decided to go there together and see what black people had to say about this. In those days we worked such trips this way. We would fly into a nearby city

—either Memphis or New Orleans. A Mississippi car, driven by black people, would pick us up and drive us to the area of trouble. We would get our answers as rapidly as possible and get gone.

But even as we were making our arrangements, the nervousness overwhelmed us. There was some flaw in the planning. We called our contact again from the airport in Chicago. Dick Gregory wanted to make sure the pick-up car would have someone he knew. I heard him shout into the phone: "I'm not going to get in a car with anybody unless I know who he is!" By then we were both trembling. We were shaken with tremors of pure fear. When I mentioned this to Dick Gregory, he mumbled, "That's what we call knee-knocking courage." I suppose almost everyone in that kind of work had to learn a simple technique: to make our wills say "yes" even when our bodies and our nervous systems said "no." It is possible to go places and to function even when you are frightened. We discovered, incidentally, that although Mr. Allen was not involved in civil rights, as the officials stated (as though that were a good enough reason for getting killed!) he had had the misfortune to witness a white man's attack on a black man and had been forced to testify to that in a court hearing the Wednesday before the Saturday on which he was found shot.

In a sense we led absurd lives in those days of terrible tensions. We formed a kind of loose confederation, without organization, exchanging information, helping one another. I deliberately did not belong to any organization. All of us, blacks and whites, were more or less in touch with one another and at the same time pretty independent. If something occurred in an area where one of us might be, particularly if it involved an injustice done to a black man, whichever of us was closest to it tried to find out what had really happened and tried to help, if possible. Because the Klan and Klan sympathizers were strong, we often stayed in the homes of brave black people. Often when I was doing investigatory work in the South, I would travel with my old friend, P. D. East, the white editor of *The Petal Paper,* one of the heroes of early resistance to racism in his southland. He was a comic genius who worked effectively by ridiculing the racists. He was broken, harassed, and impoverished because of this. But even in tragedy he was irrepressibly funny. One day we were driving through a particularly disturbed area of the South where the Klan was strong. We were very nervous for fear someone would recognize us. In those days, strange things happened. Police cars, for example, would simply get behind you and trail you so that you did not dare call on the person you intended to see for fear he would receive reprisals later. Filling stations, service stations, were particularly adept at spotting suspicious persons and reporting them to the police or highway patrol. The police could stop you on any pretense—you were going too fast, or you had broken some law—and question you and harass you. Since so many of the lawmen were racists, it could be a nerve-wracking experience. I forget where we were going that day, but we were driving through a beautiful forest on a good highway and I heard P. D. begin to curse under his breath. We were driving very carefully so as not to attract attention. I looked back and saw a police car, or perhaps a highway patrol car. In a moment the car began to flash its dome flasher. We had to stop.

"Let me do the talking," P. D. growled.

"I won't open my mouth," I said.

We waited, almost paralyzed with fright. Both of us were extremely hated in that particular area.

The officer approached the driver's window of the car and asked P. D. where we were going.

In a voice of humble cordiality, P. D. gave him some response.

The officer replied with greater warmth, said we had made a turn back there without flashing the turning lights. Relieved that he apparently did not recognize us, we began testing the turning lights and found one of them did not work. He said he would not ticket us, but we should get it fixed at the next stop. P. D. thanked him profusely and we drove on down the highway, watching in the rear view mirror to see that the patrol car was not following. It turned and headed in the opposite direction and both of us heaved sighs of loud and profound relief.

"That was a close one, Griffin," P. D. said. "Did you see

how cool I was in handling him?" P. D. asked this brashly, in complete contrast to his mild and meek manner with the officer.

"You were great, P. D.," I said. "Let's hurry up and get out of this part of the country. The next one might recognize us." He accelerated slightly and we drove on in silence as I watched the tall trees flash past the car windows.

Suddenly P. D. exploded. "Why, that ignorant sonofabitch. That insulting, *ignorant* sonofabitch!"

"What're you talking about, P. D.?" I asked.

"Do you realize that ignorant bastard didn't even recognize us? Hell, Griffin, we're famous, and he didn't even recognize us. I'm insulted."

"You'd better thank God he didn't."

"Well, I do thank God he didn't," P. D. said, "but that doesn't make it any less insulting."

In spite of everything, however, those days of the early and mid-sixties were full of hope. The country seemed to be awakening to the depth of injustices suffered by black people. Hundreds of college students, white and black, poured into black areas to register black citizens for the vote. In areas outside of the South, students on campuses were deeply concerned and picketed local businesses that continued the practice of discrimination. These events became a matter for world news coverage. The world watched and mourned the bombings of Birmingham. The world watched, outraged and inspired by the events at Selma, enthralled by the Washington March. A major civil rights bill was passed in 1964, and if it was controversial, it at least nullified a lot of local discriminatory ordinances.

This great surge of concern was important but it was also deceptive. Many white civil rights advocates did not keep in close touch with the reality being lived by black Americans. For example, the noted Ralph McGill, Pulitzer Prize-winning author and editor of the *Atlanta Constitution,* did a major article for *Look* Magazine in which he stated that the civil rights battle had been won. It was all over. Only a few diehard bigots were left, he said. Everything was rosy.

I was in Atlanta when that article hit the newsstands. McGill had been highly respected by black people. I visited several of the black scholars in the universities that day, including Dr. Benjamin Mays and Dr. Samuel Williams. All who had seen the article were stunned, embittered, and outraged by McGill's totally unrealistic and misleading statements—stunned that a man of his impressive credentials could be so out of contact with truths that almost any black man could have told him.

The truth is that if things looked beautiful to whites sympathetic to the movement, this was a surface appearance. What lay beneath the surface was another matter. It is true that hope and determination now largely replaced the old despair and that was in itself a tremendous advance. But still the problems of daily living for the vast majority of black men had not yet changed. Black people were still fired from their jobs for daring to register. Economic discrimination was rampant all over the land. The black press covered many events and developments that were never mentioned in the white press. To get anything like a full picture, you had to read the black press. It was revealing to see how few whites did. Again and again, in lectures to universities with good social science departments where students were fired with enthusiasm for racial justice, I found that the school libraries, which took every newspaper and magazine published here and in Europe, did not have any subscriptions to black newspapers, scholarly journals or magazines. We were already a land of two peoples (more, of course, but we are concerned with two here) possessing two entirely different sets of information, and we were out of touch with one another.

The situation was doubly dangerous because we thought we were, finally, communicating. We were not, of course, because even well-disposed white men tended to be turned off and affronted if black men told them truths that offended their prejudices. For years it was my embarrassing task to sit in on meetings of whites and blacks, to serve one ridiculous but necessary function: I knew, and every black man there knew, that I, as a man now white once again, could say the things that needed saying but would be rejected if black men said them. In city after city we had these meetings to attempt to communicate, and in each one my function was to say those things that the black men knew much better than I could hope to know, but could not communicate as yet for the simple reason that white men could not tolerate hearing them from a black man's mouth. Dick Gregory and I once made an experiment with this. We agreed to say essentially the same things to a lecture audience at the same school. I got an ovation for "talking straight." He got uncomfortable silence for saying the same things.

Another time, this was eloquently illustrated in a small community where there had been much tension between Protestants and Catholics. A professor of Bible at a local college persuaded the two groups to get together and sponsor a lecture by me. I went in and lectured precisely on these problems of communication. I went into it in great detail. The audience, as always, thought I was talking about somewhere else and was sure it was "different" there. At the end I got a prolonged standing ovation. Afterward I went to a reception for the whites who had promoted the lecture and one black guest. We were introduced. I was told in his presence just how proud the community was of its black industrial psychologist and how he had "gained acceptance" in the most perfect way. The professor of Bible who had initiated the project was jubilant. He remarked loudly what a great success it was and how marvelous that the Protestants and Catholics had finally worked together to make it a success.

"I view this as a historic night," he announced. Then turning to the black industrial psychologist, he asked, "Don't you see this night as a historic turning point for this community?"

The black doctor, in a voice of perfect calm, replied, "Frankly, I'm not too excited."

The Bible professor's face clouded, and he said, "What do you mean?"

The doctor said, "It's true that I have a good job in this town, and I seem to be respected, and I am certainly paid a wage commensurate with my skills. *But*—so long as I have to house my wife and children in a town twenty miles away because I can't buy, rent, lease or build a home here, don't expect me to get too excited over your 'historic turning points.'"

I watched, fascinated, as the group of whites began to

growl and the professor of Bible reddened with anger. "Well, I'll tell you one thing," he said. "If you're going to be that cynical, I don't see how you can expect us to do anything for you."

I heard a local minister mumble to a lady standing beside him, "I knew there'd be trouble if we invited that black man. . . ."

The Bible professor lost most of his self-control. He battered at the lack of graciousness and courtesy that he perceived in the black doctor. The doctor remained calm, lethal in his replies, unshaken.

I watched until the professor was almost screaming his anger and then stepped in. "Isn't this remarkable?" I said. "Here you gave me a standing ovation for telling you this same kind of truth. Now you have a black man, far more knowledgeable than I could be, who is honoring you with a truth, and you are furious with him. You will hear it from me and applaud me for saying it, but you can't stand it yet from him."

The point was finally made, but I doubt if it would ever have been made if that doctor had not been invited and had not spoken up.

Almost constantly and almost everywhere black men were being faced with this kind of duality. Whites were saying the right things, showing deep concern over injustices, expressing determination to resolve the problems of racism, but never really consulting with black people as equals. The vast difference between what this country was saying and apparently believing, and what the black man was experiencing, was embittering.

As a person who lived almost constantly in both communities, I could forsee nothing but trouble. Frequently, in cities where "racial difficulties" surfaced, I was called in by perfectly sincere community leaders, usually mayors or college presidents or city council members. They wanted me to study their situation and report to them on it. First I would have meetings and be briefed by white men, often by trained white social scientists. Then I would be taken into the black community, where again I would be briefed by black leaders and sometimes black social scientists. In no city did these two briefings coincide. In St. Louis,

Rochester, Detroit, Kansas City, Los Angeles, and many others this occurred. In every city there was this different view of the same situation by perfectly sincere men. I always pointed out the irony in this: I was being called into an area I did not really know. Why not ask local black leaders directly the kind of questions the cities were asking me? After the first difficulties in Rochester, New York, I was asked to consult with community leaders. I went and spoke for quite a long time. The leaders were concerned and sincere men. The first question one of them asked after I talked was: "Well, Mr. Griffin, what is the first thing we should do now?" I told him that I had been asked to come and consult with community leaders, and yet I was sitting in a room full of white men. Rochester is full of knowledgeable black men. The white man who had asked the question slapped his forehead in real chagrin. "It never occurred to me to ask any of them," he said apologetically.

"So you see what's happening," I said. "Black men are going to know about this meeting. I have already consulted with many black men locally because that's the way I get my information. See how it looks from their point of view. You have brought me a long distance to consult with community leaders about a problem that profoundly involves black men in this community, and yet no black man was invited." I warned them that this kind of thing was interpreted by black men as part of the hopeless lack of understanding on the part of white men and that they must be careful to invite men the black people considered leaders, not just a few black men that the business and community leadership considered leaders.

Later, I got a call from one of the white leaders who asked: "How do we go about finding black leaders whom the black people would respect as leaders?"

"Ask black people—ask a lot of black people," I advised.

This kind of pattern existed almost everywhere. I would be called in. Often in the presence of local black men whites would ask me questions that should have been addressed to the black men present. They knew the community, I didn't. Always this was an affront to black men, one of the many affronts that white men apparently could not perceive. What it really told black men was that we had better buckle down and garner the superior problem-solving abilities of white men to get this thing settled. This is one of the attitudes that led black men to believe that racism was so deeply engrained in the white man there was really no hope of his ever understanding. This was an attitude, too, which did not inspire one bit of confidence in black men who saw problems affecting their very lives being handled by white men who did not even consult with black men.

So, while on the surface, things looked good and promising to white men, and I was always being urged to admit that great "progress" had been made, resentments grew among black people, and quite particularly among educated black people.

Black spokesmen like Dr. King, Roy Wilkins, Whitney Young, James Farmer, Dick Gregory, Stokely Carmichael and many others warned that the inner cities were becoming powder kegs and would certainly explode. In every city I was brought in to study (and often I returned again and again) I would live in the black ghetto with black families, and I would come out and give the most detailed analysis to the whole city and to community leaders, warning them that black resentments and frustrations were explosive and that one day some little insignificant event would occur and produce an explosion that would astound the whole community.

In every city the local community leaders who had brought me in nevertheless felt that they lived there and knew better and said that I was being "unduly pessimistic." In some cities I was called "unduly pessimistic" only weeks before the explosions occurred. And when those cities exploded into turmoil, men who had not believed me would telephone to tell me I had been right and they had been wrong.

"I wish I had been wrong," was all I could answer.

One of the strange things was the resentment people showed when you gave such warnings. The warnings were seen as threats. Often I was accused, as were even Dr. King and Dick Gregory, of *advocating* violence. This is like accusing a doctor of advocating the very cancer he is trying to prevent from spreading. But somehow people could not face what appeared inevitable, and they sought to evade it by viewing these warnings as threats.

And when the matches were tossed and the powder kegs began to explode in 1967, men hid behind the belief that it was all some massive subversive plot against this nation. The Kerner Commission was established and asked to investigate. Its report, which was a courageous one under the circumstances, showed that matches had indeed been tossed and the powder kegs had exploded—and that these were individual explosions, not connected through any discernible subversive plotting on the part of black men. The Commission report warned that massive displays of force in so-called riot control was one of the deepest sources of resentment and could trigger off more riots. The report was an obvious disappointment to some of our leaders, who had really counted on it to reveal massive subversion, so they simply cast its recommendations aside with the remark: "The report blamed everyone but the rioters." Black spokesmen countered by saying that to blame the rioters would be like blaming the powder keg that exploded.

This was perhaps the most terrible time in modern history insofar as civil rights were concerned in this land. Black people began to believe in greater numbers that this country was really moving toward genocide, and from the point of view of black America, the evidence was alarming. That year, in President Johnson's State of the Union message, his appeals for social justice and civil rights met with absolute silence from Congress—not a single lone handclap of approval broke that silence. His appeal for saving the California redwood trees, which followed immediately, got an ovation of wild, handclapping approval from Congress. The message was clear and desolating. It showed this country's priorities and mood. It said to every black man: "Save the redwood forests and to hell with you."

In my dismay, I wired the President: "AM TIRED OF BEING A LOSER. FROM NOW ON I'M GOING TO FORGET HUMANITY AND WORK FOR THE TREES."

The patterns of the exploding inner cities began to

emerge. From the black man's viewpoint it often looked as though black people were being driven to a flare-up which would then justify suppression by white men on the grounds of "self-defense."

In those terrible days of open conflict, I was being taken into the inner cities, usually by black militants, as an observer. I hardly ever opened my mouth. The day was past when black people wanted any advice from white men. I was taken in simply to view it from the inside, so that in the event we did come to open genocidal conflict, there would be someone to give another view to history. And another view I got. I attended enraged meetings where black men, women, children, students, discussed their experiences. Everyone was saying the turmoil was the work of young blacks. That was not true. Middle-aged and elderly black people attended those meetings everywhere, and burned with rage. In Wichita, Kansas, I heard a young college student say the kinds of things that were being said in all the cities. He recounted an injustice done him in that community. He showed wounds where he had been beaten by white men.

"We've tried everything *decent*," he said loudly.

"Yes," the audience responded. "Yes. Who can doubt that?"

"We asked for justice and they fed us committees," he shouted.

"Yes."

"They've even got committees to decide how much self-determination we're going to have."

"Take ten!" someone shouted from the back of the room.

"Take ten!" a few responded.

After he had spoken, the young man came over to my chair, almost sobbing with frustration. He looked into my eyes with eyes that were wild with anguish and whispered while we shook hands, "When you go back, will you do me a favor?"

"Yes, if I can," I said.

"When you go back out there, will you tell your friend, Jesus Christ, and your friend, Martin Luther King—

'shit!' " He spat out the word with the deepest despair I have ever heard in a human voice.

On the streets, young black men would call out, "Take ten!" to one another. Whites thought they were talking about a ten-minute coffee break. What they were really saying was that this country was moving toward the destruction of black people, and since the proportion was ten whites to every black, then black men should take ten white lives for every black life taken by white men.

Certainly the news reports and coverage, given largely by white interpreters outside the ghettos and widely and sincerely believed by horrified whites, had no credibility within the ghettos because they did not coincide with what black men were experiencing; and in the heat of emotions, few white men could penetrate the troubled areas, and the media had not yet hired many black reporters who could have given a more balanced view.

As black men began to compare notes with me around the country, a strange pattern began to emerge. If it did not hold true for all the exploding communities, it held true for many of them. In these, someone in a high place—the mayor, chief of police, or other official—would receive information that a neighboring city was already in flames and that carloads of armed black men were coming to attack this city. This happened in Cedar Rapids when Des Moines was allegedly in flames. It happened in Ardmore, Oklahoma, and in Ft. Worth, Texas, when it was alleged that Oklahoma City was in flames and carloads were converging on those two cities. It happened in Reno and other western cities, when Oakland, California, was supposed to be in flames. It happened in Roanoke when Richmond, Virginia, was supposed to be in flames. And in many other communities. In no instance were these reports true or were any of these cities actually in flames. But the result was immediate action on the part of the white officials. They got in contact with important community and industrial leaders. Riot control measures were ordered into effect. Civilians armed themselves for the coming attack and stationed themselves at strategic points. In most cases many whites became aware of the "danger" and no local black person had any idea of what was going on, though I recall one case where the rumor spread through a west coast community and a white official called a young black teacher with whom he was friendly. He told the black teacher about the report and asked him to look around the neighborhood and see if anything suspicious was going on—any preparations for battle. The young black man went and looked and returned to the phone. "It looks pretty sinister," he said. "There's a lady across the street putting her baby in the stroller, and down the block I saw a man mowing his lawn. You'd better take proper precautions."

In most cases, however, black people were quite unaware that a storm was brewing. Then, when the riot controls had been put into effect, and a nervous white population was waiting, it took little to set it off. In Wichita, a few white youths drove down into the black area and simply fired off guns. This brought black people out of their houses; in rage at seeing the harassment, they hurled stones or sticks at the passing car, and the battle was on. In that particular instance the police arrested the five whites who were armed and twelve young black men who had only rocks and sticks. All were jailed. The next morning, all were released on bail, but the bail set for the five armed whites was only one-fifth the amount set for the twelve unarmed black students. This kind of overt inequity in bonding spread its message to the black community. And when no whites protested, or even seemed to find it unjust, black people saw that as highly significant, too.

In other cities, it was enough to throw rocks on the porches of black people to bring them out and for the confrontation and the madness to occur.

Some cities were saved. Variants of this rumor-mongering set off other cities.

Who was doing this? I don't suppose anyone really knows. White people were sure it was traveling black agitators who came in and exploded the community from within. Black people viewed this as an open lie, since the explosions occurred from outside the ghettos; also they were not seeing any "traveling black agitators," at least until after the explosions had happened. And certainly no one had to come in and stir up resentments among black people in 1967—these resentments were open and raw already.

In not a single one of these cities where the hundreds of carloads of armed blacks were supposed to be converging did any of these cars show up. How did it happen, black people asked, that white people did not notice this and repudiate the pattern of rumor? In Davenport, Iowa, officials were informed that a busload of armed black men were coming in from Washington. The police alerted civic leaders and went to meet the bus. There was indeed a busload of black people from Washington, but they were not armed. They were teachers on tour.

Again, we had the duality of viewpoint regarding who was actually implementing these patterns of tension, rumor and explosion. Black people were absolutely certain it was not black people, and it was generally feared it might be some white racist group and therefore another symptom of genocidal manipulation. I traveled from city to city in those days, and the view from within the ghettos was terrible and terrifying. While white people in the periphery were arming themselves against the day when they would have to defend themselves from attack by blacks (and really believed someone was fomenting a racial war in which black people would rise up and attack them), black people mostly without arms huddled inside the ghettos feeling that they were surrounded by armed whites. Black parents tried to keep a closer watch on their children. Black men spoke of the old "licenced blood lust" which allowed racists to do anything to black people and get away with it.

Local white leadership was discredited in the eyes of black people, too, by their insistence on asking me, when we met to discuss the local events, usually with black people, if I had discovered who was the traveling black agitator who had come in and stirred up their "good black people." And had I discovered if there were any communists behind the disruptions? Black people just could not believe local white officials, who surely must be aware of local conditions, could really think the explosion had been caused by "outside agitators" or communists. And the white officials were viewed as completely insincere. Sadly enough, I knew the white officials really and sincerely did believe the causes lay elsewhere than in their own backyards.

During the Miami Republican Convention of 1968, because the media had black reporters who could get into the black area even in crisis times, this whole nation saw the making of a riot unfold before them on TV screens. They saw the unwarranted police raids on black political caucuses because these caucuses refused to allow white reporters. They saw a curfew that was ordered in the afternoon when most black people were at work or did not have their radios on. They saw that curfew really being made known for the first time to most black people that evening when law enforcement men rolled into the black areas, unleashed a cloud of tear gas, and only then announced on their portable speakers that a 6 P.M. curfew had been ordered and all people should return to their homes and stay inside. After that series of provocations, the city exploded into a riot. The country saw it, got a good and expert report on it. The commentators even mentioned the fact that it was very hot and the people were cooling themselves outdoors, since there was little or no air-conditioning in the dwellings of that part of the city. And yet, within hours, one of the state's top officials blandly announced that they were looking for the communists and black outside agitators who had caused it. Presumably they never found them. Black people who had witnessed this all over the country could only despair at the gullibility of white people who, seeing all this, swallowed the old line that it was caused by communists and black agitators.

Three weeks before the assassination of Martin Luther King, I met on the West Coast with a group of black leaders to compare notes. Almost simultaneously, many black people had become convinced that every time a black community was goaded into such an explosion, it served only the cause of racists and brought us closer to a genocidal situation. The word went out not to let racists goad the communities into flare-ups. This is certainly one of the reasons why Dr. King's murder did not unleash massive violence, as might have been anticipated. There were, of course, scattered pockets of retaliatory violence in some of the Eastern cities and Washington, D. C., but it was not the all-out race war that it could have been.

What reconciliation was possible then? If whites looked on blacks with distrust, it was nothing compared to the vast distrust with which blacks regarded whites.

Almost ironically, the person of Martin Luther King in life and in death became the touchstone for a whole new evaluation among black thinkers. This evaluation led to alternatives to violent confrontation. So, in a bizarre sense, Dr. King, who had seemed so defeated and who had died without much hope that his philosophy of nonviolent resistance had accomplished anything, became the mainspring for a whole new way of thinking among black people and, in the long run, averted violent head-on collision between the citizens of this country. As a result of this new thinking, the "take ten!" call faded. Black men began to see other ways out. A whole new dynamism was put into play at the time of Dr. King's martyrdom.

Up until that time black thinking had been focused on the dream of an integrated society as the ultimate solution to discrimination and racial injustice. It was a dream held also by many whites, a dream for which many whites and blacks had already died. This dream was so deep, so cherished, and seemed to be such an unqualified good that no one really questioned it. It took men of great mental toughness to begin to ask if that dream had not carried in its wake certain weaknesses for the black American. When this painful line of thought was opened up, it became apparent that at least some of that dream had kept black men weak. For example, if a black man set up a business, he might very well hear his black potential clients say: "After all this struggle for integration, I'm not going to self-segregate," and refuse to patronize his business.

Also, it was generally believed, though the belief was fading, that most "good whites" lived in the North and most "bad whites" lived in the South. Certainly many northern cities deplored what was going on in the South. But when Martin Luther King, who had been so praised in the North for the work he did in the South, came to work in the cities of the North, the very officials who had praised him sometimes led opposition to his work locally.

This revealed to black people that there was no basic difference between attitudes in the North and South. A white-imposed separation had always existed in both areas. Dr. King's trips into the North showed that even in the friendliest cities there would always rise up out of the local community sufficient opposition to prevent bridging this separation. It became bitterly apparent that this separation was going to go on existing into the foreseeable future.

What then? Black leaders and thinkers began to stand back and review the situation. Their conclusions were harsh. The old dream, and the constant hope for one solution—that of an integrated society—had not worked and had little chance of working now. Black people were jammed together in ghettos and were going to have to stay there. All the apparent progress had not changed the problems of black people living in the ghettos of this land. Black men were still not able to function as men, as leaders of their households, as self-determining and self-respecting human individuals. What were the possible alternatives to these exhausting and violent cycles of hopes built up and then dashed through the moods of white society?

Black leaders pondered. They must find the genius to turn a seemingly hopeless situation into an advantageous one. The first step was to accept the realities of the situation and act on them rather than on some nebulous dream of a future when all men would come to the realization that racial justice was for the good of all society, not just for the good of the oppressed.

Once viewed from this perspective, some startling facts became clear. Black thinkers, discarding the old dream, began to expose the weaknesses that had been built into the system. The first of these weaknesses was called "fragmented individualism" by the philosophers. As soon as it was defined, it was understood by black people and recognized. What fragmented individualism really meant was what happened to a black man who tried to make it in this society: in order to succeed, he had to become an imitation white man—dress white, talk white, think white, express the values of middle-class white culture (at least when he was in the presence of white men). Implied in all this was the hiding, the denial, of his selfhood, his negritude, his culture, as though they were somehow shameful. If he succeeded, he was an alienated marginal man—alienated from the strength of his culture and from fellow black men, and never able, of course, to become that imitation white man because he bore the pigment that made the white man view him as intrinsically other. The instant the term fragmented individualism was understood, it was completely understood by black men who had lived it in all its nuances. And as soon as it was understood, black men could do something positive to counter it. The "brother" and "sister" concept swept in. Black people deliberately stopped trying to imitate white men in dress, speech, and etiquette. Black men reversed the weaknesses of fragmented individualism by studying black history, developing black pride, even using words like "black" which had been oppressive before, hammering them home until they stood for the symbol of the New Black and became beautiful.

Black thinkers spoke of turning the ghettos into gardens, taking over their own schools, building a "nation within a nation."

They pointed out the economic weaknesses of the old system. Most businesses in black areas were owned by white men, particularly the big chain grocery stores. Black people were shown that their dollars lost strength when spent in those stores because the profits went into white banks, which would not discriminate against black people for TV and car loans, but would discriminate against them for small-business or housing loans. With this understanding, black people in Chicago began to make the rounds of such stores, saying in effect that if the stores expected to sell another leaf of lettuce to black people, the stores had to hire black personnel, including black people at management level; and furthermore, they had to bank the proceeds of that particular ghetto operation in black banks which would not discriminate against black people in loans. The stores had to comply, and this was so successful in Chicago that the techniques spread across the country.

At more personal levels, it began to be understood, and was then quickly understood, that black society must work to salvage the black male child. Always before there had been concern for the black girl child. It was now pointed out that the black male child, even in a black school using white textbooks, could early come to the conclusion that all the heroes in history were white men. Furthermore, with the exception of nationally known black civil rights leaders like Martin Luther King, Roy Wilkins, James Farmer, and others, the black male child frequently saw the adult black male as ineffectual and defeated. The old picture of the white man leading the black man by the hand toward the solution to his problems again gave the black male child a view of the adult black male as something not worth becoming, and killed his spirit and his will to become an adult, problem-solving individual. This perception swept the nation. Black parents began to demand changes in textbooks and to demand that black people be visibly involved in the solutions to all problems that concerned them. A few white men who had worked long and hard in civil rights saw the immense importance of this new perception. Men like Saul Alinsky and Father Groppi and others, who were regarded as heroes of the civil rights movement, began to fade from public view, although continuing to work privately. They felt, as many blacks now felt, that for the sake of that black male child, black men should be seen as the problem-solvers and leaders, and that whites should stay out of the spotlight.

Some whites, who had never really understood, were offended by this sudden death of their role as the "good white leading the poor black out of the jungle." Many of these were among the saddest people of our time, good-hearted whites who had dedicated themselves to helping black people become imitation whites, to "bringing them up to our level," without ever realizing what a deep insult this attitude can be.

White perception of these rapid changes in black concepts lagged. Whites, in general, could not keep up with the progress of black thinking. It was fascinating and tragic to see so many whites who had given long years to civil rights work suddenly excluded from the thinking of black men. Black students were particularly aware that they had to give the black child a view of black men standing on their own, and to erase all hints of the old view of being led by whites. College students formed black student unions and excluded white students. Few white students understood. White college students, after all, had been one of the great bulwarks in the battle for racial justice, and many had dedicated themselves heroically to this cause. But part of that incipient racism had always led whites to assume the leadership positions and perpetuated the view that whites rather than blacks were the heroes of the movement. Really sincere and informed whites were thanked for what they had done and advised to go and work in their own communities, to combat the racism there which could ultimately be as oppressive to non-racist whites as to blacks. Some did this and continue to do it, though it is perhaps more onerous than working with blacks.

The same principle held in black universities, where students demanded more and more black teachers. White professors who had virtually dedicated their lives and their academic careers as historians, anthropologists, sociologists, to the problems of racism and its cures, thinking they did this for the good of the oppressed victims of racism (and often suffering social and academic insults as a result), were asked to leave schools in favor of black teachers. Some of them turned very bitter.

Some who were eminent authorities in their disciplines, and were recognized as such by black authorities in the same disciplines, were told by students that their work was not relevant because they were not black. To have one's life's work dismissed in such a frivolous manner by people who have never yet studied it was a severe insult. One elderly scholar who had been a thundering advocate of civil rights now speaks of "those black punks." Another, a sociologist, still involved in the study of discrimination in medicine and medical schools, recently told a professor at a California medical school who was proud of the achievement of black medical students there, "Well, I hope when you get sick you call one of *them*."

Such men, deeply offended to be excluded from participation with black men in the solutions to the problems of racism, sometimes begin to look for symptoms of inferiority as a means of self-defense. We are seeing a recrudescence of these contentions by scientists, even to the recent suggestion that men with lower IQs (by white-oriented tests) be paid to have vasectomies—one thousand dollars for each point lower than 100, so that a man with an IQ of 90 would get ten thousand dollars to have himself sterilized. This has been viewed as another example of genocidal thinking.

All of this is part of the current scene. Some people call it polarization, and many of us, white and black, still remember the days of the early and mid-sixties when we were all working together, singing "We Shall Overcome" and thinking that success was just around the corner.

But now, though we can still bungle into fratricide, there is really more hope than in the past. In the past, hope was based on the moods of the majority—a fragile and slippery basis. That is gone now, and a realism—harsh, full of contradictions—has replaced it as something more solid on which to build, a basis which says that black people will continue to move toward being fully functioning and self-determining people. And this is irreversible.

Polarization. Separation. No one has wanted this, white or black. It has come because the things we dreamed of did not materialize. Many still hold the old dreams even while accepting today's realities.

A couple of years ago I was seated in an auditorium in Detroit where Reverend Cleage was explaining to a conference of priests that what they called "black separatists" were in reality men who recognized the implacability of a white-imposed separation.

Afterward, one of the priests got up and asked: "But aren't you advocating an un-Christian way—the way of accepting as a reality this white-imposed separation? You are a minister. Are not all of us who are ministers obligated to bring men together in love?"

"Yes," Reverend Cleage said. "And because you have not preached that long enough and loudly enough, we are faced with accepting the separation."

Eventually, some black thinkers believe, this "separation" may be the shortest route to an authentic communication at some future date when blacks and whites can enter into encounters in which they truly speak as equals and in which the white man will no longer load every phrase with unconscious suggestions that he has something to "concede" to black men or that he wants to help black men "overcome" their blackness.

Recommended Reading from MENTOR and SIGNET

☐ **FROM FUGITIVE SLAVE TO FREE MAN: The Autobiographies of William Wells Brown.** Edited and with an Introduction by William L. Andrews. This unique volume gives contemporary readers a rare glimpse of the most prolific and multifaceted African American author of his era. "Historically more important to the development of negro literature than any of his contemporaries."—J. Saunders Redding   (628608—$4.99)

☐ **THE COLLECTED STORIES OF CHARLES W. CHESNUTT. Edited and with an Introduction by William L. Andrews.** This important collection contains all the stories in Chesnutt's two published volumes, *The Conjure Woman* and *The Wife of His Youth and Other Stories of the Color Line*, along with two uncollected works: the tragic "Dave's Neckliss" and "Baxter's Procrustes," his parting shot at prejudice.   (628438—$5.99)

☐ **THE AFRICAN-AMERICAN NOVEL IN THE AGE OF REACTION: THREE CLASSICS. Edited and with an Introduction by William L. Andrews.** Includes *Iola Leroy* by Frances E. W. Harper, *The Marrow of Tradition* by Charles W. Chesnutt, and *The Sport of the Gods* by Paul Laurence Dunbar—novels that remain significant as works that influenced a nation's conscience.   (628497—$5.99)

☐ **NARRATIVE OF THE LIFE OF FREDERICK DOUGLASS:** *An American Slave* by Frederick Douglass. Preface by William Lloyd Garrison. One of the most eloquent indictments of slavery ever recorded, revealing the inhumanity suffered by slaves in the pre-Civil War South.

(161882—$4.99)

Prices slightly higher in Canada

There's an epidemic with 27 million victims. And no visible symptoms.

It's an epidemic of people who can't read.

Believe it or not, 27 million Americans are functionally illiterate, about one adult in five.

The solution to this problem is you... when you join the fight against illiteracy. So call the Coalition for Literacy at toll-free **1-800-228-8813** and volunteer.

Volunteer Against Illiteracy. The only degree you need is a degree of caring.